Today's Army Spouse Experiences In Garrison

Problem Solving, Resource Use, and Connections to the Army Community

THOMAS E. TRAIL, CARRA S. SIMS, KIMBERLY CURRY HALL

Prepared for the United States Army
Approved for public release; distribution unlimited

RAND ARROYO CENTER

For more information on this publication, visit **www.rand.org/t/RRA429-1**.

About RAND

The RAND Corporation is a research organization that develops solutions to public policy challenges to help make communities throughout the world safer and more secure, healthier and more prosperous. RAND is nonprofit, nonpartisan, and committed to the public interest. To learn more about RAND, visit www.rand.org.

Research Integrity

Our mission to help improve policy and decisionmaking through research and analysis is enabled through our core values of quality and objectivity and our unwavering commitment to the highest level of integrity and ethical behavior. To help ensure our research and analysis are rigorous, objective, and nonpartisan, we subject our research publications to a robust and exacting quality-assurance process; avoid both the appearance and reality of financial and other conflicts of interest through staff training, project screening, and a policy of mandatory disclosure; and pursue transparency in our research engagements through our commitment to the open publication of our research findings and recommendations, disclosure of the source of funding of published research, and policies to ensure intellectual independence. For more information, visit www.rand.org/about/principles.

RAND's publications do not necessarily reflect the opinions of its research clients and sponsors.

Published by the RAND Corporation, Santa Monica, Calif.
© 2021 RAND Corporation
RAND® is a registered trademark.

Library of Congress Cataloging-in-Publication Data is available for this publication.
ISBN: 978-1-9774-0728-3

Cover: Photo by Sgt. Mike Alberts.

About This Report

This report documents research and analysis conducted as part of a project titled *Exploring the Qualities and Impact of Army Spouse Resource Use*, sponsored by the Assistant Chief of Staff for Installation Management, U.S. Army. The purpose of the project was to explore the qualities of Army spouses' resource use at the garrison level, the relationships across that resource use, spouses' attitudes toward the Army, their support for staying in the Army, soldier and family characteristics, and actual retention of soldiers over time.

This research was conducted within RAND Arroyo Center's Personnel, Training, and Health Program. RAND Arroyo Center, part of the RAND Corporation, is a federally funded research and development center (FFRDC) sponsored by the United States Army.

RAND operates under a "Federal-Wide Assurance" (FWA00003425) and complies with the *Code of Federal Regulations for the Protection of Human Subjects Under United States Law* (45 CFR 46), also known as "the Common Rule," as well as with the implementation guidance set forth in U.S. Department of Defense (DoD) Instruction 3216.02. As applicable, this compliance includes reviews and approvals by RAND's Institutional Review Board (the Human Subjects Protection Committee) and by the U.S. Army. The views of sources utilized in this report are solely their own and do not represent the official policy or position of DoD or the U.S. government.

Contents

Tables

Summary

The U.S. Army provides many resources to help soldiers and their families cope with major life events associated with Army service, such as moves associated with new assignments or deployments, and resources that can help with the day-to-day needs of military families. Although these resources are available to all Army families, services or programs are administered at the local level through community-based services or through Army garrisons. However, families can have difficulties finding the appropriate resources and accessing them. The research discussed in this report examines the experiences of Army spouses in navigating the resource system to find the help they need to address a wide variety of problems. Because the Army community can serve an important role for Army families, we focus in particular on whether these experiences vary across garrisons and the connections that Army spouses make with each other and the Army community as a whole, as well as how these connections foster better resource navigation and more effective resource use.

The research team used a mixed-methods approach to examine Army spouses' problem-solving processes and the role of the Army community, supplementing quantitative analysis of previously collected results from the Today's Army Spouse Survey, fielded in 2018, with additional qualitative interviews of 42 Army spouses who had participated in that survey. An earlier report detailed the overall findings from the survey (see Trail, Sims, and Tankard, 2019), and the current survey data analysis explores whether spouses' problem-solving processes and experiences of the Army community differ across garrisons, including the most pressing challenges spouses face, needs associated with those challenges, use of resources to receive help with those needs, and whether or not their needs were met. The semistructured telephone interviews focused primarily on spouses' experiences with Army resources and programs and the Army community.

It is important to keep in mind that the survey was not originally designed to acquire a large, representative sample of spouses *at all Army garrisons* within the continental United States (CONUS) (i.e., the study did not sample more spouses from smaller CONUS garrisons to increase representation of those locations), so the experiences of spouses at some garrisons or stationed outside the continental United States (OCONUS) are not represented in the results. In addition, although the qualitative interviews enabled us to probe deeply into the detail of individual spouses' experiences, we spoke in depth with only about 40 of them—too few to be representative of the population of Army spouses.

Findings

A number of themes emerge from our assessment of survey results and interview discussions, which help point to areas where the system could be improved:

- **Our primary finding from the analysis of survey data is the commonality of spouse experiences across garrisons** in terms of the problems they experienced, their needs for help with their problems, the resources used to help meet those needs, and whether their needs were met by those resources. We analyzed survey data to explore whether spouses' experiences vary at different garrisons across CONUS. Similar to findings for soldiers (Sims, Trail, Chen, Miller, Meza, et al., 2018), results suggest more uniformity than difference across garrisons. The differences that were observed generally do not form a pattern that suggests systemic differences in the experience of Army spouses navigating the resource landscape, although spouses at Fort Benning reported higher levels of social support from their military network and more positive attitudes toward the military.

- Both survey findings and interviews illuminate **the challenges many spouses (as well as their soldiers) experience in navigating resources, and that some spouses experience getting "bounced around."** Based on survey findings, it is common for spouses to seek help in solving problems through multiple resources, regardless of location, and some needs go unmet. Those who participated in interviews related stories of being referred to multiple resources to get help. These referrals were sometimes perceived positively by spouses as a way to get the appropriate type of help but, in some cases, referrals were described as hitting dead ends, resources they were referred to could not help them and they had to start over in their search for resources, and they were bounced from one resource to another, which suggests that warm handoffs to appropriate resources were not always the norm.

- When we asked interview participants what would improve their ability to find resources, the spouses we interviewed spoke of the **utility of a "one-stop shop"** that serves the function of providing an entryway to help locate resources. This suggests that some spouses are not familiar with existing formal resources, such as Army Community Service (ACS) and Military OneSource, which are intended to serve such a purpose. Availability and awareness of a one-stop shop for locating resources is especially important, since many of the spouses who reported using multiple resources had Army-specific problems.

- According to our interviewees, **Army spouses find information about the resources available to them most frequently from other Army spouses**, whether through social media or in person. Interviewees also appreciated multiple modalities of contact, such as engaging through social media and using pamphlets distributed on garrison that identify available resources. Spouses suggested a number of ways to improve resource information sharing, such as a comprehensive welcome session and a centralized information repository for local installation resources.

- Interviewees identified ACS and Army Family and Morale, Welfare, and Recreation (MWR) as **programs perceived as having positive reputations; these could serve as gateways to other programs for spouses**. Accessibility; streamlined processes; helpful, welcoming, and well-informed staff; and affordability were identified as characteristics of programs that spouses perceived as having a positive reputation.
- **Connections with other spouses are helpful for a range of reasons:** as social connections, guides to military life and culture, sources of information about available resources or services, and useful entry points when arriving at a new location. Many interview participants reported feeling engaged with other Army spouses; some interviewees said they would appreciate greater connection with the Army community.
- **Not all Army spouses interviewed want greater connection.** Some reported being too busy with other commitments (including civilian employment) to want or need a higher level of engagement with the Army community. Moreover, many interview participants reported that their connection varied over time and context. Living in smaller communities or communities with a high concentration of Army families tended to result in closer ties, as did life events such as having children.
- **Connections offer an opportunity to alleviate the challenges of military life.** Despite the natural ebb and flow of the need and desire for connection, Army resources and, more generally, social contact with the Army community have utility and are connections the Army should help facilitate for families in need.

It is important to note that most of the qualitative interviews were conducted before the COVID-19 pandemic disrupted military and civilian life (i.e., before mid-March 2020). The shutdowns of schools and military childcare, as well as potential delays in permanent change of station (PCS) moves and loss of employment for spouses, could have created major problems that spouses needed to address. We reason that the issues facing interview and survey participants are likely to continue regardless of the pandemic (e.g., spouses will likely continue to have difficulty navigating the military resource system), and some existing issues are likely to be amplified because of the pandemic (e.g., the experience of loneliness and the need for connection to others in the Army community). Thus, we conclude that our main findings will continue to be valid in the postpandemic world. However, we have modified our recommendations somewhat to address potential changes to the status quo (e.g., in-person welcome sessions were desired by spouses, but they may not be feasible if physical distancing restrictions continue to be needed).

Recommendations

Our findings suggest that, for the most part, challenges facing spouses and their experiences navigating the resource landscape are common across the Army. As with the general resources provided (ACS, Child and Youth Services, MWR, and others), this suggests that a common Army approach implemented locally is a reasonable one to take. It is clear from our previous work (Sims, Trail, Chen, Miller, Meza, et al., 2018; Trail, Sims, and Tankard, 2019); the expansive literature on social support demonstrating the positive benefit of additional instrumental, informational, and emotional support for coping with challenges (e.g., Cohen and Wills, 1985; Taylor, 2011); and the interviews conducted for this report that connections to the Army through other Army spouses serve to increase awareness of and access to military and civilian resources to help spouses find help for their greatest problems and needs. In this way connections serve as a gateway through which spouses can avail themselves of the benefits of being part of the Army community, though the current study does not assess the use or effectiveness of these resources. The bulk of our recommendations, described below, are designed to expand those gateways or enhance the current gateways for spouses:

- **Soldier and Family Readiness Groups (SFRGs) should be leveraged as a means to inform spouses of what is available and should continue to provide a venue for connection with the Army community when such connection is desired.** Survey and interview data suggest that Army spouses did not often identify Family Readiness Groups or SFRGs as a source of help for challenges, though many interviewees reported that they were engaged with an SFRG, at least tangentially. However, SFRGs serve as a potentially useful social support function because they are uniquely positioned to help Army spouses engage with each other and can serve as a gateway to the Army community. As a result, they have utility for helping spouses resolve the problems they experience. *We suggest that SFRGs incorporate organized activities beyond SFRG meetings, such as sports or games, to encourage social connections among spouses.*

- **Provide welcome sessions just for spouses who have recently moved to a garrison, ideally conducted in person.** Some spouses interviewed reported challenges finding a gateway to learn about available resources, echoing a survey finding that Army spouses often have difficulty navigating the military resource landscape (Trail, Sims, and Tankard, 2019). One way the Army can introduce spouses to SFRGs and other gateways to the Army community is by conducting strategically planned welcome sessions just for spouses who have recently moved to a garrison. These sessions would potentially serve as a gateway to the available resources themselves, through the provision of information about the garrison and local Army and civilian resources, but they would also offer a venue whereby spouses new to the garrison might be able to connect with other similarly situated spouses. For example, *connections could be fostered through a spouse mentor or buddy system that is organized and centralized at the garrison and by gathering spouse email addresses at the session to form a garrison-specific listserv.* When provided, these sessions should be scheduled at a time and location that is convenient for spouses and, when possible, conducted in person. Some garrisons are already doing this, but a more systematic approach may prove helpful to the Army.

- **Develop a website where spouses can follow up on resources described during an initial welcome session.** An initial welcome session would not be sufficient to provide spouses with all the information about the resources available to help them, especially given their different preferences for connection to other spouses and their preferred mode of connection (i.e., in person or online). Moreover, spouses may not need the flood of information presented to them at welcome sessions until they are faced with a problem. Interview results suggest that a convenient resource, such as an up-to-date website that details available resources, would extend the utility of welcome sessions for the duration of spouses' tenure at a given location.

- **Consider incorporating formal, interactive online activities providing connection and social support to Army spouses, such as moderated online forums specifically for those seeking help.** Spouses interviewed reported reaching out to other spouses through informal Facebook spouse groups, and earlier survey results suggest that Facebook is one of the most preferred gateways for spouses to get information about the resources available to meet their needs (Trail, Sims, and Tankard, 2019). A more formal online gateway that still provides interactive help to spouses could be one way to reach those who live far from the post and desire greater connections to the Army community, but it could also be a gateway to better connections for spouses who reported that they did not want to directly connect with other spouses. A moderator would exert greater control over the content of online forums and provide greater support for spouses who need help and an alternative online gateway to the Army community.

- **Use resources such as ACS and MWR as avenues to provide spouses with information on the range of problem-solving programs available to them.** Interviews suggest that Army spouses do view these resources, particularly ACS, as a one-stop shop for information. Our findings suggest that bolstering this role further has utility.

- Spouse interviews reinforced previous survey findings suggesting that even spouses who are relatively connected to the Army community sometimes have difficulty accessing and navigating the Army system (Trail, Sims, and Tankard, 2019). To ameliorate the difficulties that spouses have in finding information about garrison resources, the Army could

  - **increase the prominence of Military OneSource as a guide to finding *local* resources and make it easier to use for that purpose**
  - **develop more consistency across garrison homepages with regard to information about services**
  - **optimize Army or other military web-based resources so that Army spouses using a general search engine (e.g., Google) to search for resources are likely to be connected with appropriate Army resources.**

- **As a best practice, ensure that warm handoffs between programs are standard rather than the exception.** As has been noted in previous work (Sims, Trail, Chen, Miller, Meza, et al., 2018; Trail, Sims, and Tankard, 2019), Army programs and leadership should establish a "no wrong door" policy through which spouses who contact them for help can be directed to the most appropriate resources for their problems, even if those resources fall outside the purview of the programs or leaders. Part of this policy should be to train leaders and program staff on the resources available to Army families and how best to refer family members to those resources (Sims, Trail, Chen, Miller, Meza, et al., 2018). Interviews suggest that sometimes spouses seek multiple resources because an initial resource will not resolve their problem. They may find other resources themselves, or their initial service provider may refer them to another resource that is believed to be more appropriate for a given problem. A best practice is that the referring provider directly link a spouse with the referred resource (i.e., a warm handoff). It is unclear whether warm handoffs in family programs are the norm, but it is clear from our interviews that some spouses have had to seek other resources on their own, without the benefit of a warm handoff. This is particularly important because interviews suggest that the need for such transfers is greatest for Army-specific problems such as PCS moves.

Although the Army offers a variety of resources to help military families solve Army-related challenges and day-to-day challenges that arise from Army life, survey results and discussions with Army spouses suggest that it is not always easy to find these resources when needed. In turn, some families are not able to get the help needed. The Army community provides gateways to foster better resource navigation and more effective resource use. Not all spouses desire greater connection with the Army community, but the research literature and the spouses themselves point to the utility of such connections, as social support serves a useful function for resolving life's troubles. The Army should take steps to further the gateways for Army spouses to increase connections with each other and the rest of the Army community, and to make it easier for all spouses to get information on available resources and identify those resources that are appropriate to their needs. Our recommendations suggest specific actions the Army could pursue.

Acknowledgments

We thank our sponsor, Daniel Klippstein, Assistant Deputy Chief of Staff, G-9, U.S. Army. We would also like to thank our action officer, Kelly (Dorie) Hickson of the Soldier and Family Readiness Division, Office of the Assistant Deputy Chief of Staff G-9, U.S. Army, who provided invaluable guidance throughout, starting with the Today's Army Spouse Survey (TASS) and continuing through this project. Richard Fafara and Joseph Trebing also provided help with fielding the TASS, coordinating with stakeholders, and connecting us with appropriate points of contact to help market the survey, as well as providing thoughtful feedback. We would like to especially thank the Army spouses who participated in the survey and the interviews.

At the RAND Corporation, Carolyn Rutter provided statistical advice, expert consultation, and guidance on how to convey the results. Linda Cottrell lent us her programming expertise and familiarity with administrative data sets. Alice Shih, Molly Waymouth, and Sarah Weilant provided help with interview facilitation, interview data transcription, and analysis.

We also thank Michael Linick, the director of RAND Arroyo Center's Personnel, Training, and Health Program during the time of our survey fielding, for his guidance and advice. We thank Heather Krull, the current director of the program, and Maria Lytell, the associate director, for their guidance and advice, as well as for their thoughtful comments on the work. We also thank Barbara Bicksler for her editorial help, and Susan Catalano and Francisco Walter for administrative assistance. Last but certainly not least, we would like to thank our peer reviewers, Sarah Meadows at RAND and Deborah Bradbard at the Institute for Veterans and Military Families, for their thoughtful suggestions on how to improve this report.

Abbreviations

ACS	Army Community Service
AER	Army Emergency Relief
CI	confidence interval
CONUS	continental United States
CPA	certified public accountant
DoD	Department of Defense
EPA	Environmental Protection Agency
FRG	Family Readiness Group
JBLM	Joint Base Lewis McChord
MWR	Army Family and Morale, Welfare, and Recreation
MyCAA	My Career Advancement Account
OCONUS	outside continental United States
PC	personal computer
PCS	permanent change of station
PX	post exchange
SFRG	Soldier and Family Readiness Group
TASS	Today's Army Spouse Survey
USO	United Service Organizations

CHAPTER ONE

Introduction

The U.S. Army provides a myriad of resources to help soldiers and their families cope with major life events associated with Army service (e.g., permanent change of station, or PCS, moves and deployments) as well as the day-to-day needs of a military family (e.g., childcare and medical care). These resources are available Army-wide, but Army families generally access resources at the local level through community-based services or programs administered through Army garrisons. Although Army resources are made available to all such families, regardless of location, family members can have difficulty navigating the numerous programs and services to find the best resources to fit their needs (Sims, Trail, Chen, Miller, Meza, et al., 2018; Trail, Sims, and Tankard, 2019). Depending on garrison location, Army families may face different problems and have different experiences navigating the Army system to get help. These differences could occur because of something inherent in the services provided by the garrison (e.g., the availability of program staff or the helpfulness of the staff), or because of something about the structure of the community of Army families at the garrison (e.g., where families live relative to the garrison, and how well the families are connected to one another versus to spouses' civilian coworkers). Despite these possibilities, a prior analysis of *soldiers'* problem-solving processes found little evidence of substantial variation in such processes across continental United States (CONUS) garrisons (Sims, Trail, Chen, Miller, Meza, et al., 2018). Notably, although the most prevalent types of needs reported by soldiers varies across garrisons, the problems experienced by soldiers and their ability to use resources to solve problems did not significantly differ across the garrisons studied (Sims, Trail, Chen, Miller, Meza, et al., 2018).

In this report we focus on the experiences of Army spouses in navigating the resource system to find the help they need to address a wide variety of problems. We particularly focus on the connections that spouses form with each other and how those connections might foster better resource navigation and more effective resource use. We also use data collected from a recent survey of Army spouses (the Today's Army Spouse Survey, or TASS) to examine potential differences across garrisons in spouses' experiences locating resources and solving problems. Given the lack of evidence of large or systematic differences in the problem-solving processes among soldiers at different garrisons (Sims, Trail, Chen, Miller, Meza, et al., 2018), the analysis of spouse differences across garrisons was exploratory, and we did not make any explicit predictions about potential differences across garrisons.

Navigating the Resources for Army Family Life

Following the terrorist attacks of September 11, 2001, the Army and the Department of Defense (DoD) increased the number and scope of programs and services available to help Army families cope with military life (American Psychological Association, 2007). The Army currently provides a wide range of programs and services to support its families. For example, childcare and child afterschool activities are offered through Child and Youth Services (CYS); family health care is provided through TRICARE; recreation and family activities are provided through Army Family and Morale, Welfare, and Recreation (MWR); and child and adult nonmedical counseling is provided through chaplains and DoD nonmedical counseling programs (e.g., Military OneSource). Furthermore, Army Community Service (ACS) provides a wide array of services for Army families, including financial counseling and assistance, pre- and postdeployment support, relocation assistance, help with spouse employment, and advocacy for victims of family violence or abuse (the Family Advocacy Program).

Although there are clearly many resources to help Army families with many different life challenges, service members and their spouses often have difficulty navigating the resource system to find the help they need. Surveys indicate that soldiers and spouses contact several different resources to find the needed assistance to resolve problems (Sims, Trail, Chen, and Miller, 2017; Trail, Sims, and Tankard, 2019), with Army spouses contacting an average of 4.4 resources per problem (Trail, Sims, and Tankard, 2019). The number of resources contacted does not suggest a simple problem-solving process.

In focus groups conducted after an initial survey of soldiers' problem-solving approaches, soldiers indicated that they did not always know where to go for help, often went to a few different resources before finding the right match for their needs, and were sometimes misdirected and rerouted through different service providers (Sims, Trail, Chen, Miller, Meza, et al., 2018). The companion focus groups with Army spouses also suggested that there is a disconnect between spouses and Army culture. Focus groups suggested that spouses' difficulty finding resources is partly the result of a lack of connection with the Army community, and particularly a lack of connection with other Army spouses (Sims, Trail, Chen, Miller, Meza, et al., 2018). Other research has suggested that social involvement helps lead to trust in the formal military support system, which in turn facilitates seeking help (Bowen, Jensen, et al., 2016).

Although previous research suggests that the problem-solving experiences of soldiers are similar across garrisons (Sims, Trail, Chen, Miller, Meza, et al., 2018), it is possible that, for several reasons, spouses' experiences navigating resources could differ across garrisons. Garrisons are situated in locations that can have very different characteristics. Some are in more urban settings, where more civilian community-based resources are available relative to rural locations. Housing can be expensive in these urban locations, however, so Army families might have to live farther from post, which would make accessing on-installation resources more difficult for spouses. Other characteristics of garrison locations could also affect housing choices, such as the quality of the local school system and the job market for working spouses in surrounding communities. In addition, garrison-specific issues could affect spouses' experiences with navigating resources, including garrisons with understaffed programs or strained resources that affect how well families can access the help they need. Thus, this report explores the possibility that spouses' experiences vary across garrisons.

The Role of the Army Community

The Army community can serve an important role for Army families, helping connect soldiers, spouses, and military children with each other to form a network of social support (National Academies of Sciences, Engineering, and Medicine, 2019). Spouses can engage with the Army community through more formal means, such as through Soldier and Family Readiness Groups (SFRGs),[1] or through more informal means, such as socializing with other Army spouses (Hawkins et al., 2018). The more engaged military spouses are with their community, the more they are able to cope with stress and be resilient (O'Neal, Mallette, and Mancini, 2018). Engaged spouses are also more likely to want their soldier to remain in the military (Burrell, Durand, and Fortado, 2003), and increased spouse perceptions of community support are associated with better family adaptation to military life (Bowen, Mancini, et al., 2003).

Social networks provide different types of social support (Taylor, 2011):

- *informational support*, such as information on upcoming family activities on post or information and advice about how the military system works
- *instrumental support*, such as help watching out for each other's children or providing a ride to the installation
- *emotional support*, such as listening to other spouses talk about their difficulties and providing validation of their experiences and assurances that they are cared for.

Formal community support programs or services can fulfill some of these support roles, such as providing information or instrumental support, but Army families can find the information to be confusing or difficult to access when needed (Sims, Trail, Chen, Miller, Meza, et al., 2018). Focus groups with Army spouses have suggested that there is a direct connection between building a network of support from other military spouses and better adjustment to Army life and Army culture (Sims, Trail, Chen, Miller, Meza, et al., 2018). Spouses report difficulty finding a network of support, especially following PCS moves or during remote assignments (Hawkins et al., 2018), and some spouses struggling to find support groups are

---

[1] Army Directive 2019-17 changed the Family Readiness Group (FRG) program to the SFRG in April 2019. SFRGs are unit-based Army support groups that provide "a network of mutual support and assistance [that] assists unit commanders in meeting military and personal deployment preparedness and enhances Soldier and Family readiness." Office of the Assistant Chief of Staff for Installation Management, 2019.

not familiar with SFRGs or have had bad experiences with SFRG events (e.g., feeling out of place; Sims, Trail, Chen, Miller, Meza, et al., 2018).

Instrumental support from formal military resources and informal social support from other spouses can be difficult to access for families who live far from the soldier's post. Military families are less likely to live in concentrated areas around military installations than they were in the past (National Academies of Sciences, Engineering, and Medicine, 2019). According to the 2015 Survey of Active Duty Spouses, 72 percent of Army spouses live off post, with 30 percent of all spouses living 30 minutes or more away from a military installation (Defense Manpower Data Center, 2016). This is important because Army spouses who live farther from post report more severe problems, have more difficulty navigating military resources, are less connected to the Army community, experience more stress, and are more likely to have unmet needs after using resources (Trail, Sims, and Tankard, 2019).

Furthermore, soldiers who live farther from post themselves report that they are less satisfied with the support they have received from Army resources, including support from their chain of command and other unit members, and they report less positive attitudes toward the Army and are less inclined to remain in the military (Sims, Trail, Chen, and Miller, 2017).

Living off post can also affect access to services for military children, and participating in military-organized youth activities promotes youth well-being (National Academies of Sciences, Engineering, and Medicine, 2019). Military children who live farther from post have higher levels of depression and anxiety and report a lower sense of self-efficacy, whereas participating in military youth activities helps children maintain relationships in the military community and is associated with less depression and anxiety (Richardson et al., 2016). In addition, living far from post and being socially isolated contribute to risk factors affecting depression and poor academic performance among adolescent children of soldiers (Lucier-Greer et al., 2014).

Taken together, these results suggest that having a support network of other military spouses is beneficial for spouse and family well-being and that having a robust source of social support is a key factor in improving resilience for military families (National Academies of Sciences, Engineering, and Medicine, 2019). Army families who live farther from post are less connected to the Army community and less able to navigate the military family resource system. They are also less likely to have positive attitudes about the military and more likely to want to leave the Army (Trail, Sims, and Tankard, 2019).

As with resource navigation, it is possible that spouses' engagement with the Army community varies across garrisons. Since how far a family lives from post can have a significant impact on its engagement with the Army community, garrisons with more on-installation family housing or with local communities with a higher proportion of Army families would foster more community engagement for spouses. As noted in the previous section, housing prices, local school quality, and the local job market can also affect where Army families live relative to the soldier's garrison. Furthermore, some garrisons may have more active SFRGs than other garrisons, and different garrisons can have different levels of other formal or informal activities to proactively engage spouses in the Army community. Although stronger connections to a community tend to facilitate greater benefits of informational and emotional social support (see, e.g., Lewandowski et al., 2011; Wellman and Whortley, 1990), connections that are more peripheral or transitory (i.e., weak ties) can also provide informational support to community members through the provision of novel information and resources (Chewning and Montemurro, 2016; Granovetter, 1984).

In this report we explore in depth how Army spouses navigate the resource system, and how they engage the military community in particular, to find the help they need. Based on our prior work, we particularly focus on the connections that Army spouses form with each other and how they rely on those connections to navigate Army and civilian resources. We also use data collected from a recent survey of Army spouses to examine potential differences across garrisons (i.e., local civilian community differences) in their experiences of problem solving.

A Review of Applicable Findings from Prior Work

The Today's Army Spouse Survey

As noted above, Trail, Sims, and Tankard (2019) fielded a survey, the TASS, to Army spouses. The survey used a unique approach centered on seeking help and problem resolution to examine the most pressing challenges that Army spouses face, needs associated with those challenges, use of resources to receive help with those needs, and whether or not the needs were met by the resources they used. This prior work examined these data at a whole-Army level, and results suggested that spouses have difficulty navigating the system of military family support programs to find the help they need. Although most spouses indicated that they were comfortable using the military resources available to them and their families, one-fourth of spouses reported difficulty finding out about military resources, and less than 35 percent indicated that they knew whom to contact if a military resource was not meeting their needs.

The analysis also found that some characteristics of Army families make them particularly vulnerable in a way that suggests that additional ties to the military might prove helpful in some cases (Trail, Sims, and Tankard, 2019). Junior enlisted spouses, spouses who were unemployed and looking for work, and spouses who lived farther away from their soldiers' military posts all exhibited patterns of vulnerability. Findings indicated that junior enlisted soldiers and their spouses are particularly vulnerable across a host of survey measures. Specifically, results suggested that these spouses were not yet integrated into the military community; they were more likely to cite problems with military practices and culture, more likely to cite a need for both general information (particularly if their problem is military practices and culture) and specific information, and less comfortable with aspects of navigating the system in place to help them. Spouses who lived farther away from their soldiers' military posts also appeared to be facing challenges integrating into the Army community; they used fewer resources overall to solve their problems; and reported lower comfort with military resources, lower satisfaction with resources, and higher levels of unmet needs. They also reported that they were less likely to be connected to other military spouses, either in person or through social media groups. Spouses who were unemployed and looking for work were more likely to experience financial or legal problems, to report needing financial help, to be less satisfied with the military and civilian resources they used, and to be more likely to have unmet needs. In contrast, spouses who had dependent children, although facing some challenges, also reported additional comfort with resources in a way that suggested that children might provide a helpful tie to integration in the military community. Our present work explores these data further to speak to differences or similarities in problem solving that may be found at the garrison level, while the overall findings reported by Trail, Sims, and Tankard (2019) characterize the predominant Army spouse experience.

A Review of Findings from Previous Garrison-Based Focus Groups

Results of a report employing focus groups of service members (and some spouses) at four installations (Sims, Trail, Chen, Miller, Meza, et al., 2018) suggest that Army families' problem-solving processes are not always straightforward. One finding that the current project builds on is that lack of knowledge about military resources, negative past experiences with resources, and inconvenient hours of operation were commonly perceived as barriers to seeking assistance. Although our focus was not on spouses specifically, those with whom we spoke expressed that they felt particularly uninformed about the military resources available to help them. Focus groups with service providers highlighted challenges in getting information to spouses about available resources, including the fact that the Army does not provide or collect email addresses for spouses. Service-member participants noted using multiple types of resources for help with problems; sometimes this was the result of being bounced around among resources before finding the correct source of help, and sometimes it was because the problems were more complex and required multiple resources. Several focus-group participants expressed the usefulness of having a central point of contact, such as ACS, to direct them to the best source of help for their problem (Sims, Trail, Chen, Miller, Meza, et al., 2018).

Although we only explored the experiences of soldiers and spouses at four garrisons via in-depth qualitative data collection, we found that the experiences of Army families were mostly similar across garrisons, and this was mirrored by soldier survey results (Sims, Trail, Chen, Miller, Meza, et al., 2018). Moreover, the most systematic way to answer the question of variance across garrisons is through appropriately collected survey data, such as those collected by the TASS. Given this consideration and the additional evidence of qualitative commonality, we did not perform a qualitative exploration of spouses' problem-solving experiences by garrison. We do, however, explore spouses' experiences with the Army community, including whether their experiences with that community varied across different garrison locations. We also explore themes found in these prior research efforts to better understand the problem-solving experiences of spouses and employ a similar mixed-method (i.e., survey and interview, quantitative and qualitative) methodology.

The Organization of This Report

In Chapter Two we describe our mixed-methods approach. In Chapter Three we detail the results of our analysis of spouses' problems, needs associated with their most pressing problems, resource use, and whether their needs were met by resources. Chapter Four further explores qualitative interview information regarding resource reputation and spouses' suggestions for improvement. In Chapter Five we consider important spousal well-being outcomes, including perceived stress, attitudes toward the military, and support for their soldiers' continuation in the Army, as well as interview findings on how spouses perceive the Army community. Finally, in Chapter Six we offer conclusions and recommendations. Appendix A contains additional survey-based analyses and results, and Appendixes B and C contain additional information about our qualitative methodology.

CHAPTER TWO

The Mixed-Methods Approach

We used a mixed-methods approach to examine Army spouses' problem-solving processes and the role of the Army community. Mixed-methods approaches offer the benefit of more generalizable results through the analysis of quantitative data, which is supplemented with qualitative methods that produce less generalizable information but provide more detailed and in-depth analysis. In this chapter we provide detail on the methodology used for the TASS (our survey) and the qualitative interviews. As an in-depth description of our survey approach is provided elsewhere, we provide only a brief description here. Interested readers can find a more detailed presentation of the survey-related sampling, weighting, and analysis in Trail, Sims, and Tankard (2019). Because the qualitative approach that we undertook is unique to this report, we cover that in more detail in this chapter.

An Overview of Today's Army Spouse Survey Methodology

As described by Trail, Sims, and Tankard (2019), and previously applied among soldiers in Sims, Trail, Chen, and Miller (2017), the TASS methodology incorporated a help-seeking and problem-resolution approach to examine the most pressing challenges that Army spouses face, needs associated with those challenges, use of resources to receive help with those needs, and whether or not the needs were met by the resources used. This relatively unique and individually tailored format of the survey allows for in-depth exploration of experiences in problem resolution. Based on a robust literature on stress and coping (e.g., Cooper, Dewe, and O'Driscoll, 2001; Folkman, et al., 1986) and family stress process models (Hill, Boulding, and Dunigan, 1949; McCubbin and Patterson, 1983), the framework of the TASS essentially parallels the coping process for dealing with problems: respondents are asked about problems they have faced, needs for help stemming from these problems, resources they have contacted for help, and the quality of their experiences using resources. The survey also assessed several important outcomes to examine how the problem-solving process was related to those outcomes. This question flow is

$$\text{Problems} \longrightarrow \text{Needs} \longrightarrow \text{Use of resources} \longrightarrow \text{Outcomes.}$$

The final question on the survey asked respondents whether they would be interested in participating in future research; if so, they were invited to provide email addresses. The final question is noted here because it was used to obtain contact information for the qualitative interview portion of our mixed-methods approach.

Survey Questions

Problems

Respondents viewed a list of 96 specific issues, grouped into nine problem domains of eight to 14 issues each, and were asked to indicate all the issues they had experienced in the past year. If none of the listed issues matched their experiences, they could write in their own. The diversity of the problem areas presented in the survey is intended to reflect the wide range of challenges that arise for spouses and their soldiers. The problem domains (with examples of specific issues) are as follows:

- **Military practices and culture** (e.g., adjusting to military language, organization, or culture; getting your spouse's chain of command to take you seriously)
- **Work-life balance** (e.g., finding time for sleep, healthy diet, and physical exercise; work not challenging or does not use skills/education)
- **Household management** (e.g., finding suitable housing or encountering poor housing quality)
- **Financial or legal problems** (e.g., trouble servicing debt or paying bills; finding a job that pays enough or offers enough hours)
- **Health care system problems** (e.g., difficulty finding a physician who takes TRICARE)
- **Relationship problems** (e.g., trouble reuniting/reconnecting after a deployment)
- **Child well-being** (e.g., lack of affordable or quality military childcare)
- **Problems with your own well-being** (e.g., feeling stressed, overwhelmed, or tired)
- **Problems with the soldier's well-being** (the same issues as "your own well-being," but with the soldier as the frame of reference).

If respondents selected issues in more than two domains, they were asked to choose the two "most significant problems" they faced in the past year. All additional questions related to problem solving on the survey were asked about these top two problems. If respondents did not select any of the provided issues and did not write in one or more of their own issues, they were asked to confirm that they had not experienced any problems in the past year. If they confirmed that they had experienced no problems, they were coded as having no problems and skipped to the outcomes section of the survey.

Needs

For each of the top two problems selected by respondents, respondents indicated what types of help, if any, were needed to deal with the specific issues in that domain. The list of types of help was the same for all problem domains and included the following options:

- General information: for example, about rules or policies, or about what is available and how to access it
- Specific information: for example, about training or deployment schedules or how spouses can reach deployed troops
- An advocate: someone to try to get help for you

- Advice or education: people with experience to recommend the best solution for some-one in your situation
- Emotional or social support
- Professional counseling
- A helping hand: loans, donations, or services to help out with some of your responsibilities
- Activities: for fitness, recreation, stress relief, or family bonding
- Other needs that do not fit into the categories above (please specify).

If respondents listed more than two types of help needed for any problem, they were asked to prioritize the top two types of needs for the problem. For each problem, they could also select "I had no need for assistance in this area." Respondents indicating no need for assistance for both of their top problems were coded as having no needs.

Use of Resources

For each of the needs associated with respondents' top problems, they indicated which resources, if any, they had "used or tried to use to meet [the] need." The list of resources was the same for all problem domains and needs, and it included multiple options for both Army and nonmilitary contacts. Army contacts were chosen from a list of 13 options that included the soldier's chain of command, the FRG,[1] a military-covered medical provider, military internet resources or official Army social media, ACS, and MWR.

Nonmilitary resources included similar types of assistance as the military contacts, though not military-specific resources such as chain of command. Respondents chose from a list of 12 potential options, including personal networks outside the military; other military spouses known in person; internet resources; unofficial social media military networks; and religious or spiritual groups or leaders.

Following the list of military resources, respondents could select "I didn't contact any Army contacts for help with this need," and following the list of nonmilitary resources, respondents could select "I didn't contact any nonmilitary contacts for help with this need." Respondents who indicated that they contacted no Army or nonmilitary resources for help with any of their needs were coded as not using resources. Finally, respondents who used resources were directly asked whether they had actually received the help they needed; they could answer "yes," "no," or "not sure." Looking across problem-need pairs, we considered spouses to have an unmet need if they said they were "not sure" that one or more needs were met, or "no," one or more needs were not met.

Outcome Variables

The TASS included measures assessing several outcome variables, including scales that use a set of related questions to assess an outcome and single questions assessing an outcome. These measures included spouses' attitudes toward their soldiers remaining in the military

---

[1] We used *Family Readiness Group*, the term predating the August 2019 change to *Soldier and Family Readiness Group* (Office of the Assistant Chief of Staff for Installation Management, 2019), as the survey fielded prior to this change.

(measured by their rating of one item: "How much do you favor your soldier staying or leaving the military?"). Using scales, the survey also assessed spouses' attitudes toward the military, perceived stress, and perceived loneliness. The majority of these variables, with the exception of loneliness and social support, are described in more detail in Trail, Sims, and Tankard (2019).

The TASS included a validated scale of loneliness (Hughes et al., 2004) that used a five-point scale ranging from 1 (never) to 5 (very often). An example item is "How often do you feel left out?" We computed the average of these three items; reliability was acceptable (Cronbach's alpha = .91).[2] The TASS also included measures of spouses' perceived levels of support from their informal military social networks (i.e., military-connected family and friends) or their informal social networks outside the military. These measures were adapted from a scale of perceived social support by Cornwell and Waite (2009). Support from their informal military social networks was assessed with two questions: "How often can you open up to family and friends within the military if you need to talk about your worries?" and "How often can you rely on family and friends within the military for help if you have a problem?" Support from their social networks outside the military was assessed using the same two questions, substituting the term "outside the military" with "within the military." All four questions were rated from 1 (never) to 5 (very often). Reliability was acceptable for the military social support (α = .92) and nonmilitary social support (α = .85) scales.

Survey Sampling and Procedure

A detailed description of the sampling plan is provided in Trail, Sims, and Tankard (2019); in brief, the sample was selected to be representative of Army spouses along several dimensions: the presence of dependent children in the household, housing location (on post versus off post), geographic location of post (urban, midsize city, rural), and soldier's pay grade. The pay grade groups were E1–E4 (junior enlisted), E5–E9 (senior enlisted), O1–O3 (junior officer), and O4 and above (senior officer). The total final sample was comprised of 75,000 spouses. Sampled spouses were invited to participate in in two waves: 50,000 were contacted in wave 1 of the survey administration (January 2018), and an additional 25,000 were contacted in wave 2 (March 2018). For additional details about the procedure and the sample, see Trail, Sims, and Tankard (2019).

Response Rate and Weighting

Of the 75,000 spouses sampled for the survey, 74,509 spouses had viable U.S. Postal Service addresses and were mailed postcards inviting them to participate in the survey;[3] our response

---

[2] Cronbach's alpha is a measure of the average association between ratings of different items (i.e., the inter-item reliability). Alphas above .80 are considered to indicate that the items are highly reliable.

[3] Note that a substantial number of postcards were returned to the survey vendor as undeliverable. We did not exclude these spouses from the response-rate calculation.

rate was 11.1 percent, or a total of 8,275 survey respondents. (For more information about the response rate, see Trail, Sims, and Tankard, 2019.) To ensure that the results presented in this report are representative of the demographics of the Army population, we weighted the data using poststratification weighting methods.

Data Analysis Approach

For the present analysis, we examined the number of responses from each garrison represented in the sample of spouses and selected the garrisons that had at least 200 unweighted survey responses for further analysis. (For a list of selected garrisons and number of survey respondents, see Table 2.1.) This follows the approach described in more detail in Sims, Trail, Chen, Miller, Meza, et al., 2018, and was done to ensure sufficient sample sizes for statistically sound comparisons throughout the survey content, which by its nature divides respondents into smaller subgroups (e.g., those who had problems with their own well-being versus who did not; those who contacted a chaplain for help versus those who did not). Although we selected specific garrisons for further study based on numbers of unweighted

TABLE 2.1

Garrisons Selected for Analysis, and Unweighted Number of Survey Respondents

Garrison	Number of Survey Respondents
Fort Benning	416
Fort Bliss	608
Fort Bragg	1,094
Fort Campbell	620
Fort Carson	542
Fort Drum	322
Fort Gordon	240
Fort Hood	696
Fort Leonard Wood	206
Fort Riley	383
Fort Sill	210
Fort Stewart	456
Joint Base Lewis McChord (JBLM)	627
Other garrisons	1,855
Total	**8,275**

respondents, we present weighted analyses in this report, and did include all respondents in our analysis.

To analyze the survey results by garrison, we reasoned that conducting comparisons between each garrison and all others would require so many statistical tests that the chances of finding a significant difference by chance would be very likely. However, adjusting for the probability of finding a significant result by chance alone (e.g., through a Bonferroni correction) would not be statistically efficient because it would be overly conservative. Another possibility we considered was choosing a reference garrison and making all comparisons with this reference (e.g., comparing all selected garrisons with Fort Bragg). We decided against this method for two reasons: (1) There is no clear option for an Army garrison to serve as a reference for issues relating to problems and needs; and (2) choosing a garrison that fell in the middle of the distribution of scores would require changing the reference garrison for every analysis, which would make the results difficult to interpret.

Thus, we chose to compare all selected garrisons with the *overall average* of all garrisons in the larger sample (i.e., including those with too few unweighted respondents to be selected for more in-depth study). This method required only one omnibus test of a garrison effect (i.e., overall, whether garrisons significantly differed from the average), and 13 follow-up comparisons for each significant omnibus effect (i.e., comparing each selected garrison with the overall mean to determine which specific garrisons were significantly different from the average). This method also provided a consistent standard by which each garrison could be judged: the average score across Army CONUS garrisons. However, we would still potentially be conducting a large number of follow-up tests (13 for each significant omnibus garrison effect), and hence took additional action to protect against type 1 errors.[4]

We analyzed the data by constructing multiple regression models comparing each sampled garrison with the overall average of respondents at all garrisons, including those not selected for comparison. Continuous measures were analyzed using multivariate linear regression models, and binary measures were analyzed using multivariate logistic regression models. Covariates included the same spouse, soldier, and family variables used in the prior survey report (Trail, Sims, and Tankard, 2019), excluding garrison urbanicity. Specifically, covariates included in the models were the spouse's employment status, the presence of dependent children in the household, housing location relative to the soldier's military post, the soldier's pay grade group (i.e., E1–E4, E5–E9, O1–O3, and O4 and above), and whether the soldier had been deployed in the year prior to the survey. Results not presented in the body of the report are presented in Appendix A.

---

[4] A type 1 error is a statistical test that is found to be significant by chance alone—a possibility when many statistical tests are performed using the same data. We minimized this possibility by minimizing the number of tests and by using more stringent criteria for significance for all analyses (i.e., $\alpha < .01$ instead of the standard $\alpha < .05$).

Interview Methodology

All spouses of active duty Army members who had participated in the 2018 TASS and indicated on the survey that they were interested in participating in future research projects were eligible to participate in telephone interviews. A random sample of these Army spouses, which included representation across pay grade groups and spouses who lived both close to and far from Army installations (as indicated on their survey responses), were asked to participate voluntarily through email invitation. It is worth noting that because the TASS was conducted in early 2018 and interview respondents were not recruited until spring 2020, the sampled population was likely systematically different from the total population of Army spouses in 2020. For example, because soldiers generally get promoted through the ranks over time, the sampled population likely had fewer spouses of junior enlisted soldiers than did the total Army population. Thus, the interview respondents were not meant to be representative of all Army spouses but instead comprise a select population. While their experiences are instructive for understanding how spouses solve problems and connect with the Army community, they may or may not be representative of all Army spouses.

The research team conducted semistructured telephone interviews with Army spouses who consented to participate between the end of January and the end of March 2020.[5] Interview topics focused primarily on spouses' experiences with Army resources and programs. A full list of interview questions can be found in Appendix B. Participants were emailed a $20 Amazon gift card as a token of appreciation for their time and information.

Interview Participant Characteristics

The 42 individuals who participated in the interviews provided background information on their households, including living situations, family statuses, and the location of the military installations where their spouses were stationed at the time of the interviews. This information is summarized in Table 2.2.

The majority of the spouses interviewed were civilians. Most respondents also had exposure to the military prior to being with their soldiers, most commonly through other family members. There was an even split between participants who had been married to their soldiers more than five years and those who had been married less than five years. Almost three-fourths of all interview participants also had children under the age of 18 living in their household.

Nearly all interview participants indicated that they currently lived with their active duty soldiers, and nearly all participants had lived in their current housing for at least six months. The two main types of housing participants lived in were military housing on post (which

---

[5] Almost all of the interviews occurred before the COVID-19 pandemic disruptions to military and civilian life (i.e., before mid-March 2020). No participants mentioned the pandemic or related issues in any of their responses.

TABLE 2.2

Interview Participant Characteristics

Attribute	Count	Percentage
Participant military status		
Civilian	33	78.6
Veteran or reserve	9	21.4
Previous military exposure		
Yes	28	66.7
No	14	33.3
Soldier pay grade		
Junior enlisted (E1–E4)	15	35.7
Senior enlisted (E5–E9)	14	33.3
Junior officer (O1–O3)	6	14.3
Senior officer (O4 and above)	7	16.7
Housing status		
Military housing on post	15	35.7
Civilian housing	27	64.3
Housing distance from military installation		
Close (10 miles, less than 20 minutes from post, or on post)	22	52.4
Far (more than 10 miles, or over 20 minutes from post)	20	47.6
Length of time in current housing		
Six months or less	4	9.5
More than six months	38	90.5
Number of years married to soldier		
Five years or less	21	50.0
More than five years	21	50.0
Currently living with soldier		
Yes	39	92.9
No	3	7.1
Children under 18 in the same household		
Yes	31	73.8
No	9	21.4

NOTE: All participants indicated that their soldiers have been stationed at their current military installation for six months or more.

included privatized military housing or military family housing on post) and civilian housing (which included both housing that is owned or rented off post and housing with family or friends). Over half of the participants indicated that their housing was close to their active duty soldiers' military installation, meaning within ten miles or a 20-minute drive of the military installation. Participants' active duty soldiers were stationed at 22 different military installations across the United States and one OCONUS.[6] All participants indicated that their soldiers had been stationed at those installations for over six months.

Interview Data Analysis Approach

Once all interviews with military spouses were completed, we uploaded detailed interview notes into a qualitative data analysis software program to enable us to code qualitative interview data to identify key themes. We also uploaded participant background information obtained during interviews into the program to allow us to analyze trends along these characteristics. We developed a comprehensive coding framework for our thematic analysis using a hybrid approach of deductive and inductive coding. Protocol interview questions guided the initial development of codes, followed by adding more detailed codes as they emerged during our analysis of the broader codes. Due to the semistructured nature of the interviews, in some cases not all participants were asked every question; in these cases, response codes were developed for participants who were asked the question. More information about our qualitative data analysis approach, including our detailed coding guide, can be found in Appendix C.

Caveats for Interpreting Interview Findings

The findings reported from our qualitative interviews are intended for descriptive purposes only and are not intended to be representative of the overall population of Army spouses or any of the subgroups but rather to illustrate the experiences among those interviewed. Although we tried to attain diversity within our sample, we spoke in depth only with about 40 spouses who, as noted above, were not selected to be representative of the total population of Army spouses. Their experiences are informative for understanding the problem-solving processes of Army spouses, but their specific experiences are their own and should not be interpreted as representative of the experiences of all spouses.

---

[6] A few participants were garrisoned at off-site locations, such as recruiting offices or medical centers.

CHAPTER THREE

Analysis of the Problem-Solving Process and Unmet Needs

In this chapter we report on how and whether spouses across garrisons differ in their approach to resolving their most significant problems (drawn from TASS results). For the quantitative analysis we present some descriptive information characterizing garrisons, but for the specific garrison comparison regressions we present only analyses that showed significant differences and do not discuss those that did not. We also discuss the qualitative insights from discussions with Army spouses into the problem-solving process in general.

Differences and Similarities by Garrison in Spouses' Problem-Solving Processes

Results from the TASS illuminate areas where respondents at different garrisons differ statistically from the overall average. These results highlight areas where a particular garrison stands out as unusual in terms of the challenges faced by spouses there or differences in the processes for coping with challenges: the needs that spouses perceive related to those challenges, patterns of resource use that may be particularly pertinent for a given location's local context, and the ability of local resources to meet spouses' needs. Results that reveal areas where no garrisons differ from the overall average suggest that local context is not significantly associated with spouses' problems or the problem-solving process.

We examine the most frequently selected issues, the top problem areas chosen, the needs reported by spouses, specific combinations of problems with related needs (i.e., problem-need pairs), and whether or not spouses who reached out to resources had their needs met by those resources.

The Most Common Issues at Each Garrison

First we turn to a descriptive summary of top issues chosen at various garrisons. As reported previously (Trail, Sims, and Tankard, 2019), across all respondents the most frequently chosen issues were their own feelings of being stressed/overwhelmed/tired within the "own well-being" problem domain (56 percent); their soldiers' experiences of feeling stressed/overwhelmed/tired within the "soldier well-being" problem domain (50 percent); loneliness or boredom (39 percent);

mood changes (feeling depressed, impatient, angry, aggressive, or anxious; 36 percent); and communication challenges with their spouses (36 percent). In addition, 35 percent of respondents indicated that they have issues within military practices and culture, with "[f]iguring out how to use 'the system'—where to go, with whom to talk to get help or information" (Trail, Sims, and Tankard, 2019). As can be seen in Table 3.1, across garrisons some of the most frequently chosen issues were very similar, relating to both spouses themselves and their soldiers feeling stressed and overwhelmed, spouses managing feelings of loneliness and boredom, and communication challenges between spouses and their soldiers. Other challenges, such as those relating to timeliness in the receipt of treatment at a medical facility (49 percent of spouses at JBLM) or finding time for a healthy lifestyle (40 percent of spouses at Fort Drum), were reported frequently at a few garrisons, but far less consistently across garrisons.

We next analyzed the percentage of spouses who reported experiencing no issues over the past year (i.e., those experiencing no problems). Overall, 5 percent of Army spouses experienced no problems in the year prior to the survey (Trail, Sims, and Tankard, 2019). We analyzed the percentage of spouses across garrisons experiencing no problems and found no significant difference when compared with the overall average.

Average Number of Issues by Garrison

Overall, respondents selected an average of 14.5 issues across problem domains. As was discussed in the "Data Analysis Approach" section of Chapter Two, we first tested whether the 13 selected garrisons as a whole significantly differed from the overall average (i.e., an omnibus test of garrison differences from average). If this test was statistically significant, we conducted follow-up comparisons to test *which* of the 13 selected garrisons significantly differed from the overall average. All regressions controlled for spouses' employment statuses, the presence of dependent children in the household, housing location relative to the soldier's military post, the soldier's pay grade, and whether the soldier had been deployed in the year prior to the survey. The number of issues selected differed significantly across garrisons. Follow-up comparison analysis revealed that spouses at JBLM selected more issues than average: 16.7 percent (99-percent confidence interval [CI]: 15.4 to 18.0 percent) versus 14.5 percent.[1] No other garrisons were significantly different from the average.

The Top Two Problem Domains by Garrison

Respondents next selected the two problem *domains* that were "the most significant types of problems" they had dealt with in the past year. The most frequently reported top two problem domains overall were work-life balance, military practices and culture, and spouses' own well-being (Trail, Sims, and Tankard, 2019). As described in Table 3.2, work-life balance

---

[1] $N = 8{,}275$. Averages were weighted to be representative of the population. CIs help convey the uncertainty that is found in any estimate. For the 99-percent CIs that we report, if we measured the same variables in the same way from the same population, in 99 percent of those samples, our results would fall within the upper and lower bounds shown.

TABLE 3.1

Percentages for Spouses' Five Most Selected Issues, by Garrison

Problem Domain	Most Selected Issues	Fort Benning	Fort Bliss	Fort Bragg	Fort Campbell	Fort Carson	Fort Drum	Fort Gordon	Fort Hood	Fort Leonard Wood	Fort Riley	Fort Sill	Fort Stewart	JBLM	Other Garrisons
Own well-being	Feeling stressed/overwhelmed/tired	51	53	55	60	60	59	57	59	52	61	49	54	63	52
Soldier's well-being	Feeling stressed/overwhelmed/tired	44	50	49	54	57	49	50	53	48	54	45	46	56	43
Own well-being	Loneliness/boredom		37	38	40	43	45	34	40	43	45	42	39	43	35
Relationship problems	Communication challenges (not enough communication/difficulty expressing feelings)	33	35	37	42	39				33			37	41	
Military practices and culture	Figuring out how to use "the system"—where to go, with whom to talk to get help or information	33	34	37				35		37		35	37		33
Own well-being	Mood changes: feeling depressed, impatient, angry, aggressive, or anxious				40	37	39		40		42				34
Own well-being	Trouble sleeping							35	38		40	35			
Health care system problems	Timeliness at a treatment facility (e.g., getting a timely appointment, waiting time for an appointment, hours or days open)	32												49	
Work-life balance	Finding time for sleep/healthy diet/physical exercise					40									

NOTES: N = 7,967. Percentages are calculated among spouses who selected one or more issues and are weighted to be representative of the population. Percentages for only the five most frequently selected issues at each garrison are presented in the table.

TABLE 3.2

The Three Most Cited Top Problem Domains by Spouses at Each Garrison

	Work-Life Balance (percentage)	Military Practices and Culture (percentage)	Own Well-Being (percentage)	Relationship Problems (percentage)	Financial or Legal Problems (percentage)	Health Care System Problems (percentage)
Fort Benning	29	26		25		
Fort Bliss	31	29	24			
Fort Bragg	34	24		23		
Fort Campbell	32	27		26		
Fort Carson	32	28		26		
Fort Drum	34		28	24		
Fort Gordon	29	28	29			
Fort Hood	32	28	24			
Fort Leonard Wood	36	30			23	
Fort Riley	29	29	29			
Fort Sill	29	24	27			
Fort Stewart	29		26	26		
JBLM	31			24		28
Other garrisons	30	25				25
Army average	31	26	24	23	19	22

NOTES: N = 8,275. Percentages were weighted to be representative of the population. Percentages for only the three most frequently selected top two problem domains at each garrison are presented in the table.

was a frequently reported top problem domain across garrisons, and military practices and culture was a frequently reported top problem domain for 10 of the 13 garrisons. Problems with spouses' own well-being and relationship problems were each frequently reported at seven garrisons. In addition, financial or legal problems were one of the frequently reported problem domains at Fort Leonard Wood, while health care system problems were one of the frequently reported problem domains at JBLM, as well as among spouses at garrisons outside the 13 specifically analyzed.

Garrison Differences by Problem Domain

Although the most frequently selected problem domains differed slightly across garrisons, when we systematically analyzed garrison differences on the frequency of reported selection of each problem domain, only two statistically significant differences emerged. The first is that compared with the overall average, spouses at JBLM more frequently reported problems with the health care system as a top two problem domain (27.6 percent [99-percent CI: 22.9 to 32.5], versus 21.7 percent on average). No other garrisons significantly differed from the average for choosing this top two problem. The second difference is that, compared with the overall average, spouses at Fort Gordon less frequently reported that relationship problems were a top two problem (12.7 percent [99-percent CI: 6.9 to 18.5], versus 22.7 percent on average). No other garrison differences from the average were significant.

Needs for Addressing Problems

The subsequent section of the survey asked spouses what needs they had as related to their problems (i.e., for their top two problems, what types of help they needed to address each problem). Overall, 18 percent of Army spouses with problems reported no need for help (Trail, Sims, and Tankard, 2019). We analyzed the percentage of spouses across garrisons experiencing no needs and found no significant difference when compared with the overall average. Among those spouses who did report needs, we next describe the specific combinations of problems with related needs (i.e., the problem-need pairs), followed by an examination of common needs across types of problems.

Overall, the most frequently reported problem-need pairs were professional counseling for relationship problems (12 percent), emotional or social support for relationship problems (11 percent), and emotional or social support for problems with one's own well-being (10 percent). As shown in Table 3.3, these three problem-need pairs were also frequently reported at each garrison. Professional counseling for relationship problems was one of the three most frequently reported problem-need pairs at 10 of the 13 garrisons, emotional or social support for relationship problems was a top problem-need pair at 9 of the 13 garrisons, and emotional or social support for problems with one's own well-being was a top problem-need pair at 8 of the 13 garrisons. In addition, there was a frequent need for specific information (four garrisons) or general information (three garrisons) about military practices and culture. Less common problem-need pairs included activities for work-life balance (Fort Drum, Fort Leonard Wood, and Fort Sill) and activities for spouses' own well-being (Fort Gordon and Fort Sill).

Examining needs *across* problem domains, irrespective of the prioritized problems faced by spouses, the most frequently cited needs for addressing problems across garrisons were emotional or social support, activities, professional counseling, general information, and advice or education (Trail, Sims, and Tankard, 2019). The general needs experienced by spouses were also descriptively similar across garrisons (see Table 3.4). Emotional and social support was a frequently cited need at all garrisons except Fort Stewart, and activities was a frequently cited need at all garrisons except Fort Carson and Fort Hood. Counseling and general information were top needs at six garrisons each, while advice was a top need at Fort Bliss, Fort Carson, and Fort Drum. Finally, specific information was a top need at Fort Gordon. However, systematic analyses revealed that there were no statistically significant differences among garrisons on the frequency of reporting any of the needs.

TABLE 3.3

The Most Cited Problem-Need Pairs at Each Garrison, and Percentage Selected

	Problem-Need Pair 1 (percentage)	Problem-Need Pair 2 (percentage)	Problem-Need Pair 3 (percentage)
Fort Benning	Relationships— counseling, 15	Own well-being— emotional support, 12	Relationships— emotional support, 12
Fort Bliss	Relationships— emotional support, 12	Military practices— specific information, 11	Relationships— counseling, 11
Fort Bragg	Relationships— counseling, 12	Own well-being— emotional support, 10	Military practices— general information, 10
Fort Campbell	Relationships— counseling, 15	Relationships— emotional support, 14	Own well-being— emotional support, 13
Fort Carson	Relationships— counseling, 16	Relationships— emotional support, 12	Own well-being— emotional support, 10
Fort Drum	Relationships— emotional support, 14	Relationships— counseling, 12	Work-life balance— activities, 10
Fort Gordon	Own well-being— emotional support, 13	Own well-being— activities, 13	Military practices— specific information, 11
Fort Hood	Relationships— counseling, 13	Military practices— specific information, 12	Relationships— emotional support, 11
Fort Leonard Wood	Military practices— general information, 16	Work-life balance— activities, 13	Relationships— emotional support, 12
Fort Riley	Relationships— emotional support, 16	Relationships— counseling, 12	Military practices— general information, 11
Fort Sill	Own well-being— emotional support, 13	Own well-being— activities, 12	Work-life balance— activities, 10
Fort Stewart	Relationships— counseling, 14	Military practices— specific information, 10	Own well-being— emotional support, 10
JBLM	Relationships— counseling, 13	Own well-being— emotional support, 10	Relationships— emotional support, 9
Other garrisons	Work-life balance— activities, 10	Relationships— counseling, 10	Own well-being— emotional support, 10

NOTES: $N = 6,449$. Percentages are within garrison for respondents who reported problems and associated needs. Since respondents could list up to two needs for each of their two prioritized problems, for a total of four problem-need pairs, percentages may add up to more than 100 percent.

Resource Use

As described by Trail, Sims, and Tankard (2019), respondents who reported problems and needs on the survey also reported whether they accessed different military and nonmilitary resources to deal with their needs. Although the vast majority of respondents reported using resources to help cope with their needs (90 percent), some respondents had problems and needs but reported using no resources to help address them. Analysis revealed that the

TABLE 3.4

The Three Most Cited Needs by Respondents at Each Garrison

	Emotional or Social Support (percentage)	Activities (percentage)	Counseling (percentage)	General Information (percentage)	Advice (percentage)	Specific Information (percentage)
Fort Benning	35	29		29		
Fort Bliss	36	31			30	
Fort Bragg	31	31	29			
Fort Campbell	38	30	28			
Fort Carson	34		32		27	
Fort Drum	34	28			32	
Fort Gordon	30	34				26
Fort Hood	31		31	28		
Fort Leonard Wood	30	31		29		
Fort Riley	38	27		31		
Fort Sill	39	33		28		
Fort Stewart		30	27	28		
JBLM	35	30	29			
Other garrisons	30	29			29	
Army average	33	29	28	28	27	23

NOTES: N = 6,449. Percentages are within garrison for respondents who reported problems and associated needs. Since respondents could list up to two needs for each of their two prioritized problems, percentages may add up to more than 100 percent. Percentages for only the three most frequently selected top needs at each garrison are presented in the table.

proportion of respondents who used resources and the number of resources used per problem did not significantly differ by garrison—that is, spouses across Army installations in CONUS were similar in their likelihood to reach out when they needed help and in the number of resources they tended to reach out to.

In addition to examining the overall proportion of spouses reaching out to resources and the number of resources accessed per problem, we examined in more detail what types of resources were accessed, which may be affected by many factors, including the type of problem, resource familiarity, and resource reputation. Of those who used resources to meet their needs, the number and type of resources used varied slightly by garrison. Tables 3.5 and 3.6 display the military resources included in the survey, along with the percentage of respondents who indicated that they accessed each resource to address their needs (respondents could choose more than one resource for each problem-need pair). There was one significant difference in military resource use among spouses at different garrisons. Compared with the

TABLE 3.5

Percentage of Respondents and 99-Percent Confidence Intervals for Military Resources Used to Address Needs, by Garrison

	Your Soldier's Chain of Command	Army FRGs	MWR	ACS	Military Employment Resources	Military Education Loans or Grants
Army average	22.5	15.0	18.7	21.4	14.0	10.4
Fort Benning	18.7 (12.4, 25.0)	12.6 (7.4, 17.7)	21.6 (15.1, 28.1)	18.0 (11.8, 24.1)	14.5 (8.7, 20.2)	8.3 (3.7, 12.9)
Fort Bliss	24.9 (19.3, 30.5)	18.0 (13.1, 22.9)	20.4 (15.2, 25.5)	22.0 (16.7, 27.4)	15.4 (10.8, 20.1)	10.9 (6.9, 15.0)
Fort Bragg	19.1 (15.3, 22.8)	15.1 (11.7, 18.6)	13.9 (10.6, 17.1)	17.1 (13.5, 20.7)	12.7 (9.5, 15.8)	9.3 (6.4, 12.2)
Fort Campbell	21.9 (16.7, 27.1)	19.3 (14.4, 24.3)	17.1 (12.5, 21.6)	23.9 (18.6, 29.2)	13.9 (9.6, 18.3)	10.9 (6.9, 15.0)
Fort Carson	24.0 (18.2, 29.8)	16.3 (11.2, 21.3)	15.4 (10.5, 20.3)	23.8 (18.0, 29.6)	11.0 (6.7, 15.4)	8.9 (4.9, 12.9)
Fort Drum	24.8 (17.2, 32.4)	16.7 (10.5, 23.0)	20.3 (13.4, 27.1)	30.1 (22.3, 37.9)	16.6 (10.3, 23.0)	13.5 (7.4, 19.5)
Fort Gordon	25.1 (16.4, 33.8)	13.5 (6.7, 20.2)	25.0 (16.5, 33.6)	27.1 (18.1, 36.0)	17.7 (9.9, 25.5)	11.3 (4.6, 18.0)
Fort Hood	25.7 (20.4, 31.0)	16.6 (12.1, 21.0)	17.2 (12.7, 21.7)	19.5 (14.7, 24.2)	12.3 (8.4, 16.3)	15.3 (10.9, 19.8)
Fort Leonard Wood	16.5 (8.4, 24.5)	13.8 (6.1, 21.5)	17.7 (9.6, 25.8)	23.4 (14.3, 32.5)	20.4 (11.7, 29.0)	8.6 (2.4, 14.8)
Fort Riley	29.0 (21.7, 36.3)	19.3 (13.1, 25.5)	19.0 (12.8, 25.2)	28.0 (20.8, 35.1)	14.3 (8.7, 19.9)	17.0 (10.9, 23.2)
Fort Sill	20.6 (10.9, 30.3)	14.3 (6.4, 22.1)	20.7 (11.5, 29.9)	20.0 (10.7, 29.2)	17.4 (8.5, 26.2)	10.8 (3.3, 18.4)
Fort Stewart	25.1 (18.4, 31.9)	15.7 (10.1, 21.2)	21.2 (15.0, 27.4)	19.3 (13.4, 25.2)	14.1 (8.9, 19.4)	9.1 (4.6, 13.5)
JBLM	26.8 (21.3, 32.4)	14.4 (10.1, 18.8)	19.8 (14.9, 24.7)	16.6 (12.0, 21.1)	10.0 (6.2, 13.7)	10.7 (6.7, 14.7)
Other garrisons	19.2 (16.2, 22.2)	10.4 (8.1, 12.7)	20.5 (17.6, 23.5)	22.0 (18.9, 25.1)	15.1 (12.5, 17.8)	7.6 (5.6, 9.7)

NOTES: N = 5,826. Percentages are within garrison for respondents who reported problems or needs and used resources. Percentages shaded in gray are significantly different from the overall average. Since respondents could list up to two needs for each of their two prioritized problems, percentages may add up to more than 100 percent. CIs help convey the uncertainty that is found in any estimate; for the 99-percent CIs that we report, if we measured the same variables in the same way from the same population, in 99 percent of those samples our results would fall within the upper and lower bounds that we report.

TABLE 3.6

Percentage of Respondents and 99-Percent Confidence Intervals for Military Resources Used to Address Needs, by Garrison

	Military Internet Resources	Military Mental Health Care Providers	Military-Covered Medical Providers	Child and Youth Services	Chaplains	Army Emergency Relief	Other Military Resources
Army average	28.8	21.1	42.5	15.9	15.2	4.5	6.5
Fort Benning	31.8 (24.3, 39.3)	22.0 (15.3, 28.7)	43.7 (35.7, 51.6)	17.1 (11.2, 23.0)	17.0 (11.0, 22.9)	3.6 (0.4, 6.9)	7.3 (3.3, 11.2)
Fort Bliss	29.4 (23.6, 35.2)	23.1 (17.6, 28.5)	44.5 (38.1, 50.9)	13.8 (9.6, 18.1)	13.7 (9.2, 18.2)	7.5 (4.0, 11.0)	8.8 (5.3, 12.4)
Fort Bragg	27.5 (23.3, 31.8)	18.2 (14.5, 21.9)	44.5 (39.7, 49.2)	12.1 (9.0, 15.2)	16.3 (12.7, 19.8)	2.6 (1.0, 4.1)	5.2 (3.1, 7.2)
Fort Campbell	25.7 (20.3, 31.2)	20.5 (15.4, 25.6)	39.1 (33.0, 45.2)	16.2 (11.7, 20.7)	16.7 (12.1, 21.4)	3.5 (1.2, 5.8)	5.3 (2.5, 8.1)
Fort Carson	27.5 (21.5, 33.4)	24.3 (18.5, 30.0)	43.4 (36.8, 50.1)	15.9 (11.0, 20.8)	16.1 (11.0, 21.1)	6.2 (2.9, 9.5)	4.9 (2.0, 7.8)
Fort Drum	32.8 (24.7, 40.9)	20.4 (13.3, 27.5)	33.1 (25.0, 41.2)	20.0 (13.2, 26.8)	12.8 (7.1, 18.5)	6.3 (1.9, 10.6)	5.3 (1.5, 9.1)
Fort Gordon	30.7 (21.5, 40.0)	24.5 (15.8, 33.2)	40.5 (30.8, 50.3)	13.2 (6.4, 20.0)	11.3 (4.9, 17.6)	3.2 (-0.2, 6.7)	7.2 (2.0, 12.5)
Fort Hood	30.2 (24.7, 35.7)	21.6 (16.7, 26.6)	43.8 (37.8, 49.7)	15.6 (11.3, 19.9)	18.6 (13.9, 23.3)	6.8 (3.7, 10.0)	7.0 (4.0, 10.0)
Fort Leonard Wood	28.6 (18.8, 38.5)	15.7 (7.7, 23.6)	33.7 (23.5, 43.9)	13.0 (5.9, 20.2)	15.9 (8.1, 23.7)	3.2 (-0.9, 7.3)	8.5 (2.2, 14.8)
Fort Riley	30.3 (23.0, 37.6)	20.1 (13.7, 26.5)	41.2 (33.4, 49.0)	15.5 (9.9, 21.2)	16.7 (10.8, 22.6)	6.0 (2.1, 9.9)	5.0 (1.4, 8.5)
Fort Sill	32.9 (21.9, 43.9)	19.4 (10.2, 28.6)	39.3 (27.9, 50.7)	14.3 (6.5, 22.1)	15.8 (7.4, 24.2)	4.9 (-0.6, 10.4)	3.2 (-1.0, 7.4)
Fort Stewart	31.9 (24.7, 39.0)	22.7 (16.3, 29.1)	43.0 (35.4, 50.6)	15.5 (10.0, 21.0)	13.9 (8.5, 19.3)	3.4 (0.5, 6.2)	7.7 (3.7, 11.7)
JBLM	26.3 (20.8, 31.7)	24.1 (18.9, 29.4)	44.2 (38.0, 50.3)	15.7 (11.2, 20.1)	17.9 (13.1, 22.7)	2.9 (0.8, 5.0)	7.1 (4.0, 10.2)
Other garrisons	28.2 (24.9, 31.6)	19.9 (16.9, 22.9)	44.1 (40.4, 47.8)	19.3 (16.4, 22.1)	12.3 (9.9, 14.7)	4.2 (2.6, 5.8)	7.4 (5.5, 9.3)

NOTES: N = 5,826. Percentages are within garrison for respondents who reported problems or needs and used resources. Since respondents could list up to two needs for each of their two prioritized problems, percentages may add up to more than 100 percent. CIs help convey the uncertainty that is found in any estimate; their interpretation is as follows: for the 99-percent CIs that we report, if we measured the same variables in the same way from the same population, in 99 percent of those samples our results would fall within the upper and lower bounds that we report.

overall average, spouses at Fort Drum more frequently reported using ACS for help with their top problems and needs (as shown in Table 3.5). No other garrisons significantly differed from the average. There were no significant differences in nonmilitary resource use among spouses at different garrisons (see the tables in Appendix A). Thus, consideration of specific resource use at garrisons speaks to the universality of the CONUS Army spouse problem-solving experience.

Spouses' Perspectives on the Problem-Solving Process

Building off our previous TASS analysis of Army spouses' problem-solving processes (Trail, Sims, and Tankard, 2019), our analysis of interview data helps fill in the picture of spouses' experiences with the resource landscape and how they address the challenges they face. As noted above, unlike our analysis of TASS data by garrison, we do not attempt to draw garrison-based inferences in this qualitative work. However, we do consider issues shown in previous research to be relevant for Army families, such as soldier pay grade and how far families live from the soldiers' garrisons. To more deeply explore spouses' experiences using military resources to solve problems, we asked interview participants to describe a recent problem they faced and how they went about trying to solve that problem. We also asked them to report the resources that they typically use when they have a problem and how they find out about those resources. The findings from our interviews are based on a small number of Army spouses who participated in the interviews and are not intended to be representative of the experiences of all spouses. Even so, their experiences are illustrative of the types of experiences that Army spouses have in the problem-solving process.

Spouses' Experiences Addressing Specific Problems Through Resources

To better understand the process that spouses undergo to solve problems or challenges, we asked them to consider one problem or challenge they had faced in the past year that they had sought help to address (i.e., in a parallel to the TASS format, we focused on a particular problem). We then asked them to walk through the process of seeking out resources to find help for the problem[2]—what type of, and how many, resources they reached out to; and if they did not receive help from resources initially, the next steps they took until they reached resolution or ultimately did not receive help.

Given the wide variety of problems discussed and the relatively low number of interviews overall, we could not analyze our interview findings by specific problem domains. Instead, we

---

[2] Note that the TASS takes an extra step to ask about generalized needs before discussing resources; for the interviews, we proceeded directly to a discussion of resources.

characterized spouses' problems as *Army-specific*, meaning a problem that is a direct result of a specific aspect of Army life; and *non-Army-specific*, meaning a problem that a spouse could face regardless of affiliation with the Army. Army-specific problems included issues with military housing, deployment-related concerns, and issues related to PCS moves. Non-Army-specific problems included personal medical or health issues, employment concerns, childcare issues, needs for counseling services, and financial issues. It should be noted that these non-Army-specific issues could be related to Army life (e.g., having employment concerns because of a PCS move) but, since military practices and culture was one of the most common problem domains spouses cited on the TASS (Trail, Sims, and Tankard, 2019), we created a parallel category of problems for the qualitative results.

Our analysis of interview data explores in more depth how spouses navigated the resource environment. We find that many participants noted reaching out to multiple resources to address the problem they described to us, though no one problem domain emerged that was characterized by this resource use pattern. Spouses contacting multiple resources for a problem did so primarily for two main reasons: (1) They were referred to another resource by a resource that was unable to help; or (2) they sought help elsewhere on their own when they hit a dead end with one resource that was unable to help them and had to start over in their search for resources. A third reason, cited much less frequently than those above, was simply that spouses chose to reach out to multiple resources as a preferred approach.

Among spouses who reported using multiple resources due to referrals from one resource to another, some had positive outcomes and some experienced frustrating outcomes. Some described a warm handoff to the resource needed, where the referring provider directly linked a spouse with the referred resource, while others struggled, feeling like they were being bounced around to multiple resources while seeking help. As a positive example, one spouse commented on receiving the services she needed through a referral:

> There is one more resource that has been helpful. In the last couple of years, I've used mental health services like counseling. And we did that through a referral, and I followed up with that. I was seeing a civilian provider with that.

Not surprisingly, being referred repeatedly (versus being referred to just one resource) led to a feeling of being bounced around. This added to spouses' frustration and dissatisfaction with the process of seeking assistance. One spouse described being bounced around with referrals in the Army medical system when dealing with her son's medical issues as a game of Whack-a-Mole, noting,

> [My son] was being bounced around from doctor to doctor and mistakes were made as to where we should go or who to be seen by. He just did not have the continuity of care.

Spouses who sought multiple resources because they hit a dead end with one and had to seek out another found the experience to be consistently frustrating. One spouse described the need to reach out to multiple resources for her housing issue when she was unable to receive the help she needed:

> The problem we faced with our housing is our biggest problem. . . . Our historic house had a lot of bacteria. We reached out to a private housing company, but they were no help at all. We reached out to an environmental housing company—that was state level—for their assistance. We also had to reach out to the EPA [Environmental Protection Agency]. We did reach out to people we knew in the community as well.

Another discussed a financial issue that required seeking multiple resources after the first options did not work out:

> They don't release any of your housing benefits until you moved out. Trying to figure out the deposits and stuff is nearly impossible. You have to get it approved through your unit, but my husband's unit won't approve it unless it's an emergency situation. We looked into the AERs [Army Emergency Relief] but our unit wouldn't sign off on it. And anywhere else where you get a private loan, most companies tell you no because either your credit isn't perfect or they aren't allowed to help interest rates. We ended up borrowing from friends and family.

Types of problems that spouses used one resource to address included issues related to childcare, housing, and finances, among others. As with problems requiring use of multiple resources, no consistent problem domain predominated for these more straightforwardly resolved problems. For most of these problems, the single resource met spouses' needs, making the use of another resource unnecessary. For example, one spouse talked about using an Army resource that met her needs:

> [My problem] was once again not being able to find any jobs. I was actively seeking out employment. I have two bachelor's degrees and plenty of work experience. I had to try a new route. I had to learn something different. I used a scholarship through MyCAA [My Career Advancement Account]. It gave me a scholarship for a personal training certificate. So, I became a certified personal trainer and I didn't ever have to pay anything.

Another described her experience reaching out for help through Facebook and immediately receiving the support she needed:

> I think the only time I ever needed help was [during a medical issue with] my daughter. I posted on the [fort's] Facebook page and two women jumped in to help out, and the FRG leader came in and helped out in the hospital to take shifts so I could go home and shower. I put on the Facebook page, like, "Hey, I am on my way to the hospital." But I needed someone to drive my vehicle to me with my newborn, because I needed to [ride in] the ambulance with my daughter. A fellow spouse said that she and her husband were on the way. And this was like, midnight. The next day . . . the FRG leader reached out to me and said they were going to take four-hour shifts so I could sleep and shower. They

brought . . . play stuff for my baby while I was consoling my other daughter. That was the most connected I felt with the Army. . . . There is an immediate trust in the military, but it takes so long to develop that trust in the civilian world.

Other spouses appeared to reach out to only one resource because it was the resource they felt comfortable with. As one spouse commented,

I work from home. I am a freelance contractor. So sometimes, there is a childcare issue, especially if my husband is in the field. So, really, just trying to figure out who can watch [my son] when he's not in school . . . I rely more on the friendships I have than on the Army resources. It's pretty cut and dry. I go to the people I trust first. I like real connections versus [the] resource of random people. I go to my friends for childcare.

Similarly, another spouse noted additional potential resources her family could have used but instead only used one resource:

Finances are our main issue. I had some struggles sometimes in paying bills. We apply for personal loans. We don't ask any money from our family, we don't try any specific military program. We just try our best to pay it off.

Where Spouses Typically Seek Assistance: Other Spouses, Army Community Service, Military OneSource, and Soldiers

Beyond spouses' experiences with resources they used to address specific problems, we also asked interview participants more generally about the resources available to them—those that they typically seek help from when facing a challenge—and how they typically get information about available resources. This question was asked to explore the processes spouses used to find help, regardless of problem domain or whether the problem was Army-specific or not.

When asked where they typically seek help when faced with a problem or challenge, spouses named a variety of sources of assistance, and many cited multiple sources rather than a single one.[3] As found on the TASS (Trail, Sims, and Tankard, 2019), spouses cited reaching out to other Army spouses for help, either to people they knew in person or via the local Facebook spouse pages. Some posted questions on Facebook spouse groups, while others simply read posted comments for relevant information. As one spouse commented,

Probably just the other wives and Facebook groups are most effective. When you go to the other wives, it is in person and online. There is an Army wives Facebook group that is a very informal group.

---

[3] We also asked interview participants if they seek assistance in the same manner when their active duty spouse or child (if applicable) has a problem. Most reported that their active duty spouses would typically seek assistance themselves, often through the unit or chain of command. Spouses with children commented that they would seek assistance for a problem their child was having in the same manner they would for a problem they were facing themselves.

Many spouses also mentioned ACS or Military OneSource as resources they typically reached out to. They reported that these resources often serve as a kind of "one-stop shop" for assistance or can point spouses in the right direction to get the help they need. One spouse stated,

> I use Army Community Service and start there. It depends on what issue you're going through. . . . They're kind of like that hub that gives you what resources you need.

Some spouses interviewed reported that they ask their active duty soldiers for help when they face a challenge and that those soldiers would either reach out to resources on their behalf or direct their spouses to the appropriate resources. As one spouse commented,

> Well, first line would be my husband. If it's something associated with military. He tries to figure out where I should go. If he's not around, I go online and do a Google search. It depends on what I am having issues with.

Spouses' responses sometimes noted that they reached out to family members who had military experience for assistance.

Spouses Typically Find Out About Available Resources Through Word of Mouth

We asked interview participants not only where they typically go for help but also how they typically find out about the resources that are available to them. Not surprisingly, spouses often mentioned multiple sources of information. Consistent with where spouses typically seek help, the most frequently mentioned information source for available resources was word of mouth from other Army spouses, either directly from individuals they know or through Facebook pages. One spouse commented on this and also raised a potential concern about using this source for resource information:

> [I find out about resources] usually by reading through other spouses' Facebook posts. . . . Obviously something you find online through another spouse may not be the correct information.

Notably, few spouses mentioned SFRGs as their source of information about available resources, often via group meetings or information sent out by group leaders.

When asked how they find out about available resources, interview participants also reported that their active duty soldier often provides information to them. For example, one spouse stated,

> My husband gets information from other soldiers and people from his unit. If he sees it's pertinent, he will share it with me.

Although word of mouth was quite frequently mentioned, it was far from the sole method through which spouses discovered information about what was available. Participants also mentioned that they receive information about available resources through advertisements of available resources and programs. These types of advertisements included email and mailing lists, flyers and pamphlets provided on post and in facilities such as libraries, and information provided at installation welcome programs or welcome information packets provided to Army spouses when arriving at a new installation. As one spouse noted,

> [Information about resources is] everywhere. The military newspaper, the commissary, the magazines that you have, the library, or they'll have things on the gate, something next to it, if you need help, dial the pound sign [#], or go to here. They advertise.

Another mentioned the welcome packet information:

> I know when we first moved in, all of the information was given to you in a welcome packet. That was nice, so you knew the basics, and to have that available.

Additionally, some interview participants commented that they found out about available resources by using Google or conducting other relevant online searches.

Assessments of Unmet Needs

Resources are provided with the intent of helping Army families manage the challenges that they face. A salient outcome to consider is whether or not these needs were actually met through resource use.

The Survey Assessment of Unmet Needs Across Garrisons

We assessed the key outcome of unmet needs among our survey respondents. Respondents who had needs and used resources to help with them were asked to indicate whether they received the help they needed. Among spouses with problems and needs who used resources, 32 percent reported having one or more unmet needs (Trail, Sims, and Tankard, 2019). As was discussed in the "Data Analysis Approach" section of Chapter Two, we tested whether the 13 selected garrisons as a whole significantly differed from this overall average, controlling for the spouse's employment status, the presence of dependent children in the household, housing location relative to the soldier's military post, the soldier's pay grade, and whether the soldier had been deployed in the year prior to the survey (i.e., an omnibus test of garrison differences from average). This analysis was not significant, meaning that the frequency of unmet needs did not differ significantly by garrison. Thus, the overall mechanics of problem solving are quite similar for spouses across garrisons. Although problems may be somewhat more local, across the Army, when faced with a challenge spouses were similarly likely to reach out, access a similar number of resources, and achieve a similar rate of success.

A Qualitative Assessment of Unmet Needs

We also asked interview participants if they had unmet needs that the Army programs and resources they were aware of did not address. Most spouses interviewed reported they had no unmet needs. Some who identified an unmet need described needing help finding employment and staying employed when having to move, including help with necessary certifications to stay employed in their professional fields as they moved from place to place. One spouse commented,

> The military has a program that helps spouses get certifications when you have to move from state to state. They offer you up to three thousand dollars to get you recertified. But unfortunately, it's only for E1 to E5s, and only for certain things. So, I am an accountant. I was not able to get any funding for a recertification for CPA [certified public accountant] even when my husband was an E5. But they would let me get certified for cosmetology school. So that was very frustrating. My profession didn't make a list of professions that were mobile.

Another noted,

> When you are overseas, and trying to look for jobs, the Army's program to do so is very bad. They give more priority to the local people to get jobs on base. And then you are doing nothing for three years.

A few of the spouses with unmet needs mentioned a desire for more mental health or counseling services. As one stated,

> [There are] limited mental health services in this area. When I tried calling a lot of the providers on the list, some of the numbers didn't work. Some didn't take TRICARE anymore. I need a specific person who can do the therapy and prescribe medicine, and that was really difficult to find. So I kind of gave up.

Summary

Some differences emerged in the examination of issues and problems across garrisons. For example, though the most frequent issues reported at JBLM were similar to other garrisons, almost half of the spouses at JBLM reported that they or their family experienced challenges with "Timeliness at a treatment facility (e.g., getting a timely appointment, waiting time for an appointment, hours or days open)," which could partly account for the significantly higher number of issues reported at JBLM. Spouses at JBLM were also more likely to choose problems with the health care system as a top two problem domain, suggesting that the timeliness and efficiency of the health care system is a particular area of concern at this garrison. However, the types and number of issues reported by spouses at different garrisons were overall very similar, as were the most pressing problem domains selected.

As the findings describe, emotional or social support was a top general need across all garrisons except Fort Stewart, although emotional or social support for spouses' problems with their own well-being was a top problem-need pair at Fort Stewart. However, based on our analyses, the needs experienced by spouses were very similar across garrisons, and there were no statistically significant differences among garrisons on the frequency of reporting any of the general needs. This suggests a need for connection that is in some way pervasive across the Army. Continuing the theme of whole-Army similarity, when we examined the specific resources spouses used for the problems discussed on the survey, there were very few differences by garrison. Moreover, the need for connection was also evident: the most common resource cited by spouses was personal networks outside the military, and the second most common was other Army spouses, for 12 out of 13 locations (see Appendix A).

Although the interviews did not address garrison differences, they did provide illustrations of some spouses' problem-solving experiences. Interviews asked participants to consider a recent problem or challenge they sought help for and to describe that process. Many spouses who were interviewed described contacting multiple resources to address a problem. Those who contacted multiple resources did so primarily for two main reasons: (1) They were referred to another resource by a resource that was unable to help; or (2) they sought help elsewhere on their own when they hit a dead end with one resource that was unable to help them and they had to start over. Among spouses who used multiple resources due to referrals from one resource to another, some had positive outcomes (e.g., they were referred to the most appropriate resource for their problem), and some had frustrating outcomes (e.g., they felt they were being bounced around to different resources or they hit a dead end and had to search for a different resource). Although the number of resources and complexity of process were not characteristic of a given problem domain, many of the spouses who reported using multiple resources had Army-specific problems. Spouses who used just one resource to address their problems did so often because that one resource met their needs or occasionally because that was a resource they felt most comfortable with.

Beyond experiences with a specific problem, we also asked interview participants about the resources they typically seek help from when facing a challenge and how they typically get information about available resources. While spouses noted a variety of resources they typically reach out to for assistance, they most frequently cited contacting other spouses for help; this was mentioned by almost half of all respondents, and it echoes findings from both the TASS and other work (e.g., National Academies of Sciences, Engineering, and Medicine, 2019; Sims, Trail, Chen, Miller, Meza, et al., 2018).

In terms of how spouses generally find out about the resources that are available to them, the most frequently mentioned information source was word of mouth from other Army spouses. This again suggests the key role of interpersonal connection in the help seeking process. Other sources of information about resources included participants' active duty soldiers and advertisements, such as pamphlets or flyers, from the resources or programs themselves.

As noted in the TASS results, garrisons did not vary in whether spouses reported that they were able to resolve their problems. During the interviews, when asked if they had unmet needs that Army programs or resources did not address, almost two-thirds of participants did not report any unmet needs. Among the interview participants who did report unmet needs, those included assistance obtaining employment or maintaining employment after a PCS move (e.g., gaining a professional certification at a new location), as well as a desire for more mental health and counseling services.

CHAPTER FOUR

Resource Reputation and Suggestions for Improvement

In this chapter we discuss further insights from our interviews regarding characteristics of the resource landscape that form the Military Family Readiness System encountered by spouses (National Academies of Sciences, Engineering, and Medicine, 2019). While in Chapter Three we discussed how spouses seek resources with regard to a specific problem and how they typically seek resources in general, here we describe findings from the interviews exploring how spouses perceive the military resources available to them. Note that these perceptions are based on a small number of Army spouses who participated in the interviews. The findings are not intended to be representative of the perceptions of all spouses, but they provide an indication of which programs or services could serve as gateways to connect spouses to additional resources (those with good reputations) and which might need to address issues that contribute to spouses' negative perceptions. We also document their suggestions for how available resources might be improved to serve them better.

Reputations and Characteristics of Army Resources and Programs

We asked interview participants if certain Army resources and programs are perceived as having a positive or negative reputation in the Army spouse community and if so, what aspects about those resources or programs contributed to their positive or negative reputations. We sought to understand what resources and programs were perceived as having positive reputations among spouses and which ones were perceived as having less positive or negative reputations. A program's positive or negative reputation among the population it serves could affect how much population members trust a program and seek it out for help. For example, spouses' perceptions of a program with a negative reputation might keep them from using a program that could actually help them. Although (as noted in Chapter Three) resources often sought for general or specific problems quite often included personal networks outside the military, other Army spouses (via online or in person) and the spouses' soldiers, this discussion inherently focuses more on available program offerings through the Army or DoD.

Characteristics and Examples of Programs Perceived as Having Positive Reputations

Interview participants described what aspects of the programs contributed to them having a positive reputation. Spouses noted that the accessibility of a program is important, meaning both that the location is easy to find and that the hours are convenient. Additionally, in terms of accessibility, they noted that a streamlined process to access a resource, with limited amounts of paperwork and a transparent process for approval, is important for a program to be perceived as having a positive reputation. Spouses also appreciated friendly, helpful program staff who can make them feel welcome. Having well-informed staff who are responsive to spouses' needs and can direct them to the correct resource if they are not able to assist themselves was also something that contributed to a program being perceived as having a positive reputation. The affordability of Army resources and programs compared with those similar in the civilian world was also something spouses mentioned as important.

Specific examples of programs identified as resources with positive reputations in the spouse community were ACS, MWR, and the United Service Organizations (USO). Many spouses described MWR-sponsored recreational activities and vacation opportunities at affordable costs and family-friendly events that they enjoyed. As one stated,

> I had a good time with MWR. I thought that was a home when I didn't have a home. The facilities need a lot of work and are really run down but programs that they had are great—intramurals, group fitness activities. The people there are friendly and are willing to connect you with anything you had questions about. MWR was a place to find a community and feel at home. They got me involved with other people that also didn't have friends or know what was going on in the area. Even though I don't have kids, I also noticed that it is very family friendly, which was great. People could bring their kids to the fitness classes. I thought that was so cool. It was a real community.

Spouses commented on benefiting from the services provided by ACS and appreciated having the kind of resource that was a good "catchall" or starting point for finding the right help. One spouse described how she had benefited from ACS services:

> ACS was good. They are a great resource. I used them when I was pregnant. They were giving out free car seats. I did the class when I was pregnant, and they were very respectful and very helpful. They gave us all the information we needed. The lady reached out to me after the class, even after my baby was born. They gave us free stuff after he was born. That was pretty cool.

Other spouse programs described as having a positive reputation included the military's MyCAA scholarship and the assistance it provides for education as well as other financial assistance programs or loans available from the Army that met soldiers' needs.[1] As one spouse stated,

> MyCAA, it's good for starting out. If you are looking for a job quickly, they offer different certification programs for E5s and below, which was good if you are trying to advance your career or get a certification.

Characteristics and Examples of Programs Perceived as Having Negative Reputations

In general, when asked to describe what aspects of programs contribute to having a negative reputation, spouses cited a number of factors. They described unfriendly and unhelpful staff that did not provide the help they were seeking. One spouse stated,

> Most complaints I've seen are just bad service culture. People who work there are unfriendly and don't have a lot of empathy, . . . They don't treat people really nicely. They don't seem very proactive.

In addition to often being nonresponsive, spouses commented that some programs were not easily accessible given their inconvenient hours. As one noted,

> We have tried to do some stuff, but it's just seems like it's never really worth it. It's not really helpful. Army offers a class, but it's in the middle of the day, in the middle of the week. So I can't go because I work. And my husband is in the military. It just makes no sense.

When asked which specific Army programs or resources tended to have a negative reputation in the Army spouse community, several interview participants reported that they did not think there were any programs or resources with a negative reputation. Of the spouses who did offer feedback on programs or resources considered to have a negative reputation, issues related to the military health care and housing systems were the two most frequently mentioned resources. Common complaints about the military health care system included difficulty scheduling appointments and long wait times to be able to schedule appointments. Here are sample comments from three different spouses about the military health care system:

> The main thing I've had a frustration with is trying to make appointments for things. It's very hard to get a person. There are very long answering services, when you get to the end of the prompt, you're still not getting to someone. Two years ago, I got pregnant a month after moving here, I got to the point where I wouldn't bother calling. I would drive to the hospital and talk to the doctor's office to make an appointment because it was too frustrating to make an appointment on the phone. That's where we've had the most frustration. As far as things people complain about most often, it's usually trying to get an appointment.

---

[1] MyCAA provides scholarships to military spouses to receive education and training in portable career fields. At the time of the interviews, the program was available to spouses of service members in the E-1 to E-5, O-1 and O-2, and W-1 and W-2 pay grades.

> I honestly think the TRICARE system could use improvement, from what I've heard. My friends, they complain about the wait time. I know soldiers get seen right away at their clinic, on base. But for spouses the wait can be a little bit longer.

> Hospital advocacy here is atrocious. I waited over eight weeks for an MRI. My appointment was canceled fifteen minutes before it happened. They told me if I don't like it, then they told me to get TRICARE select. They don't do their jobs.

The spouses who identified military housing as having a negative reputation raised concerns about the poor quality and condition of military housing provided and a lack of responsiveness by the program to maintenance requests. One spouse stated,

> Housing is the only thing that is really bad around here. So a lot of the houses have mold, and a lot of them have sewage backups. This lady's house has been flooded nearly five times. Housing isn't really respected. People don't want to admit there's a problem. . . . Every time I called for help, people would clean the air duct, but I can still see the mold.

Another commented,

> The resource that I noticed is the maintenance people. They don't put in the work orders on time. They half do the work orders. . . . We had a busted pipe, and it was a big smell, and they were supposed to fix it, but the smell never went away when they said they fixed it. They finally came back and actually fixed it, which meant they never fixed it the first time they came.

Programs with Mixed Feedback

Two Army programs or resources—childcare and SFRGs—were identified by some spouses as having positive reputations, while others cited these same programs or resources as having negative reputations.[2] One spouse noted the positive aspects of SFRGs:

> I've only had good experiences. I would say communication is good in FRGs. And also unconditional support. They don't make excuses not to help you.

Another described her negative experiences:

> FRG has that bad reputation. They're mostly run by the higher ranked spouses, one of those things where personalities clash. If you're new to the military and that's your first take, it's enough to put you off of it.

Approximately equal numbers of spouses mentioned military childcare as a resource with a positive reputation or a negative reputation. Respondents who noted that childcare had a negative reputation discussed quality of care issues, long wait times, and complicated application processes at the Child Development Center. Spouses who perceived childcare as a resource

---

[2] Respondents referred to "FRGs" in their comments rather than "SFRGs." It is unclear if they were specifically referring to the previous FRG model or if were simply using out-of-date terminology.

with a positive reputation noted benefits such as affordable childcare compared with the civilian sector and convenient hours that aligned with Army schedules.

Suggested Improvements to Army Resources and Programs

Building on spouses' impressions of Army programs, we asked interview participants how the Army could improve its resources and programs to better meet their needs or make spouses more likely to use them. It is worth noting that several spouses suggested resources that are already in place, at least at some installations (e.g., resource packets for families new to an installation), but their comments are useful for understanding how these resources could be better delivered to Army spouses. We also asked interviewees how communication about Army resources and programs could be improved to better inform military spouses of the support available to them.

Several respondents suggested providing comprehensive welcome sessions or information packets when spouses arrive at a new installation. They recommended that this include information about local resources and programs available to them and how to access those resources and programs. Some spouses noted that soldiers receive in-processing when arriving at a new assignment and that a similar in-processing just for spouses would be beneficial. One spouse stated,

> I think if, when you first get here . . . I know the soldiers go through processing through the unit. I think it would be helpful if they took maybe a day to guide the spouses through an in-processing the same way and then provide them with the resources that are pro-vided at the unit or at post from the army. I feel that's a disconnect. The spouse then has to depend on another spouse, it's a lot of word of mouth, then the husband doesn't tell the spouse. So maybe incorporating, maybe if it's just a day or an hour, a brief for the spouses to go through.

Some spouses explained that they did receive a welcome packet of information, while others did not experience this at their installations, suggesting that this resource is either not consistently delivered across installations or that it is not always effectively delivered to spouses (e.g., it is given to soldiers who may or may not pass it on to their spouses). However, spouses who did receive welcome packet information still felt there was a lot of room for improvement to the way the information is provided and would prefer an in-person orientation. One spouse commented,

> Just because I am new to the area, we were new to the area, new to the military, it would maybe be nice to have some kind of welcome to base orientation or something. Not just a giant packet of information that . . . I'm awful, but I never look through those. It's a big old help book my husband brings home—what fun readings to do. If there was something like—to get to know the military installation, these are the things we offer. Something in person. Something personal like that. If they had that a few times a year. If you PCS'd here in the last few months, you're invited.

Another specific recommendation for improvements that respondents offered was the creation of a centralized repository for local installation resources. Spouses complained that there is not—or they did not know of—a single location or website to go to that outlines all available resources, and that they are left to track these relevant resources down individually and often on their own. One spouse commented,

> Every station or base have their own managing everything, and there's no one uniform website that lists everything—or at least I don't know about it. There should be a website that lists everything for each base.

Another stated,

> I think just having, on the webpage, an area that has ongoing resources in the area, especially for those that don't live on post . . . having someone to keep an upkeep on that page. . . . I think having a link on the main website of each installation for all the resources, for quick access, would be beneficial. And having someone always maintaining that.

Most spouses preferred that this proposed resource be a website rather than an in-person office, and some suggested that the website have search capabilities that would point them to the resources most relevant for them. One spouse suggested creating a smartphone app for military spouses that would allow them to choose their location and would then provide resources in that area. Spouses did not mention using the installation program directory available through Military OneSource, which lists military program contact information for every military installation worldwide (Military OneSource, undated). But it was clear from their recommendations that they wanted a website that listed local community, as well as military, resources.

Other communication-related improvements respondents suggested included improvement in marketing and promotion of available resources and programs to make more spouses aware that they exist. Respondents discussed a variety of ways to improve on pushing out this type of information. Some believed more emails should be pushed out to all spouses, allowing them to opt out but not requiring them to opt in to receive information. Some would like to be able to specify the type of information they would like to receive based on their life situation. For example, spouses with children may wish to receive information about resources for children, while for spouses without children this information may clutter inboxes and keep them from noticing communications about resources they would be interested in. Other respondents cited social media as a good way to get the word out about available resources and programs. Additionally, spouses commented that improvements could be made to Army websites in terms of their usability. As one noted,

> Army resource websites should be more user friendly. You have to use a PC [personal computer] to access them or sometimes have your husbands' military ID. It's really hard to access online resources.

A few also noted that communicating resources for spouses via the active duty member is not always effective. Many spouses prefer receiving this information directly and not having to rely on their active duty soldier to remember to pass it along to them. As noted earlier, soldiers do not always convey information about military resources to their spouses. As one spouse commented,

> A lot of the younger soldiers don't tell their wives all things that are available, so they don't know what is available. When they get indoc [indoctrinated into the Army], they get all this information about resources, but they don't tell their spouses at all.

Beyond improvements focused on communication, respondents also suggested a few program-specific improvements. These included providing more childcare options so that spouses can take advantage of classes or other resource sessions in addition to ensuring that hours for events or classes offered are inclusive to all lifestyles—that is, that they are available weeknights and weekends as well as weekdays. A few spouses cited a need for more affordable and available childcare options more generally. One spouse stated,

> Childcare is also a big thing for spouses, and many spouses are waiting on applications for childcare on base. That's a big thing; they need that. Make childcare more accessible and affordable. I know many want to work and go to school, but it's impossible. Soldiers aren't rich. They can't pay more than five dollars or six dollars an hour for childcare.

Additionally, a few spouses commented that customer service could be improved for Army resources and programs. As one noted,

> I guess just friendly atmosphere, the people who are running those programs, they need to remember that we're people too. Their job is to serve. Some of them are rude. If they could work on that aspect, being willing to help. It looks like you're bothering them because you're asking them to do their jobs.

A few respondents noted that the Army should do more to help spouses navigate resources when their active duty member is deployed. One commented,

> They have a lot of great resources for spouses and families, but I do think they need to have some better programs to help with deployment and separation. They have programs but, in this area . . . but they actually don't have any ability to provide any sort of help. They refer you to another program, who refers you to another program. You are still not getting anything out of it. It's sometimes not even worth it to try those resources. This family advocacy program does the same, it just pushes you from one program to another. There is no specific resource.

Another spouse described a need for an easy go-to resource to help with small issues that come up while active duty members are deployed.

Finally, a few described the need for improved programs to assist spouses with employment. This included help with licensing and certifications across states and ensuring that job fairs and other career services are geared toward broader, more diverse careers than are currently supported by military education and employment programs. One commented on the need for the Army to focus on the new paradigm of Army spouses' needs that include supporting their employment and career goals:

> The military spouse community is changing. And I don't think resources are keeping up with the new population that military spouses are. The resources are in a mind-set that is really archaic and what it was to be a military spouse previously—basically, a stay-at-home mom. Now military spouses are women with careers; we can't be moved every year or two years. We are losing opportunities to have a decent salary. Resources are more for conflict resolution, or a stipend to pay for *X, Y, Z*, but not helping us keep jobs. We are educated career-driven people as well. And we have to put that aside to support our spouses' careers. It is unfair.

Summary

Resource use is not solely dictated by resource availability. Comfort, familiarity, and reputation all influence whether or not a customer base will actually seek help from resources. As it can be hard to determine how factors such as reputation influence the process of seeking help, we chose to address these issues with a discussion regarding reputation in our interviews. The Army spouses we interviewed most frequently identified ACS, MWR, and the USO as resources with positive reputations in the military spouse community. They described programs with positive reputations as being easily accessible and having helpful and well-informed staff. When asked to discuss Army resources and programs with negative reputations, some participants stated that they did not believe there were any such resources or programs. Of those participants who did cite programs with negative reputations, the military health care system (somewhat echoing the garrison comparisons for JBLM) and housing systems were mentioned most frequently. Factors contributing to negative reputations included unresponsiveness of programs, unhelpful or unfriendly staff, and difficulties accessing resources. These findings echo prior work (Sims, Trail, Chen, Miller, Meza, et al., 2018), and perceptions that a program with a negative reputation might keep spouses from using resources that could actually help them. This suggests that addressing these perceptions—either directly through faster response turnaround or less directly by explaining resource constraints that preclude adding staff responders—might alleviate some concerns for spouses. The perceptions of interview respondents are not intended to represent the views of Army spouses in general, but they are suggestive of the programs or services that are viewed positively, and thus could be gateways to connect spouses to additional resources, as well as which programs might need to address issues that contribute to spouses' negative perceptions.

We also asked participants how the Army could improve its resources and programs to better meet their needs and how communication about Army resources and programs could be improved to better inform military spouses of the support available to them. Although spouses may have been unaware of all of the programs available to them, and not all of their suggestions may be viable, they do present the Army with information regarding how the Army could help them navigate the resource landscape. Respondents suggested providing comprehensive in-person welcome sessions specifically for spouses or providing information packets about local resources directly to spouses when they arrive at a new installation. Beyond improvements focused on communication, they also suggested a few program-specific improvements, such as more available and accessible childcare, improvements to resource navigation specifically for spouses during active duty member deployments, and general customer service improvements.

CHAPTER FIVE

Spouse Well-Being and Connections with the Army Community

Prior research has shown that connections with the Army community can make a difference in the ability of military spouses to access needed resources and gain needed support; it is this that we consider in this chapter. The TASS included an assessment of various measures of spouse well-being and connection to the Army. Our interviews investigated spouses' connections to the military community in more depth, probing their engagement with other Army spouses and the Army community in general, as well as their connections with other spouses made through the Army SFRGs. Although the interview results are not meant to be representative of all Army spouses, they do illustrate the ways in which spouses can connect with the Army community and their perceptions of those connections.

Differences and Similarities by Garrison in Spouse Well-Being and Connections with the Army Community

Understanding how spouse well-being varies across garrisons is important for identifying garrisons where they might need additional support from the Army to maintain readiness. In addition, spouses' connection to the Army community is an important predictor of soldier retention. We thus examined garrison differences among the survey outcomes of general attitudes toward the military, support for soldiers staying in the Army, perceived stress, and loneliness. We also examined levels of support received from spouses' informal social networks both inside and outside the military.

Examining general attitudes toward the military, we found a significant difference among spouses at different garrisons. Compared with spouses at all garrisons (average = 0.0), spouses at Fort Benning reported more positive attitudes toward the military (mean = 0.12 [99-percent CI: 0.03 to 0.21]), and spouses at Fort Carson (mean = −0.15 [99-percent CI: −0.24 to −0.07]), Fort Hood (mean = −0.10 [99-percent CI: −0.18 to −0.03]), and JBLM (mean = −0.14 [99-percent CI: −0.22 to −0.06]) reported significantly fewer positive attitudes toward the military.[1] Spouses across garrisons did not significantly differ in attitudes toward retention.

We also found a significant difference among spouses at different garrisons for perceived stress. Spouses at Fort Carson reported significantly higher levels of perceived stress compared with the average across all garrisons (mean = 2.48 [99-percent CI: 2.383 to 2.568] versus 2.379, respectively).

Examining spouses' reports of loneliness revealed a significant difference among garrisons. Spouses at Fort Bliss reported lower levels of loneliness compared with the average across all garrisons (mean = 2.59 [99-percent CI: 2.47 to 2.72] versus 2.73, respectively). Additional analyses of reports of loneliness appear in Appendix A.

It is possible that some of the solutions to these challenges of loneliness and isolation lie in connection with the community. Although connection with the local civilian community is potentially important, as long as spouses and their soldiers remain in the Army they have a potential community of support and connection available to them in the broader Army community. We thus analyzed garrison differences on spouses' levels of support from their informal military social networks (i.e., military-connected family and friends). A significant difference among garrisons emerged. Compared with the average across all garrisons (mean = 3.237), spouses at Fort Benning reported greater support from their informal military social networks (mean = 3.42 [99-percent CI: 3.243 to 3.587]), and spouses at Fort Gordon reported less social support (mean = 2.95 [99-percent CI: 2.73 to 3.18]). Additional analyses of spouses' level of informal military social support appear in Appendix A.

An analysis of garrison differences in levels of support from informal social networks outside the military was not significant. This suggests that there was something particular about the Army spouse community at Fort Benning that was associated with greater military community support and more positive attitudes toward the military—at least at the time of the survey. Additional analyses of spouses' levels of support from informal social networks outside the military appear in Appendix A. We next describe the qualitative interview data assessing spouse informal and formal social connections to the Army community.

Interview Results on Connections to Other Army Spouses and the Army Community

We asked interview participants several questions about their connections with other Army spouses, both broadly and through engagement with SFRGs, and with the Army community overall.

---

[1] As described by Trail, Sims, and Tankard (2019), the items comprising the attitudes toward the military measure were assessed on different scales (i.e., either 1 through 7 or 1 through 5), so the scale items were transformed to have a mean of 0 and a standard deviation of 1 prior to calculating the average score among items. This means that the overall average is 0, negative scores fall below the average, and positive scores fall above the average.

Connections with Other Army Spouses

When asked to describe the degree to which they felt connected with other Army spouses, many interview participants reported feeling engaged with other spouses, while the remainder noted little to no engagement. Of those spouses who reported feeling engaged, participants noted commonalities that led to this engagement, with many mentioning connections because of their children or interacting with other spouses who were neighbors. For example, one spouse commented,

> I have a couple of ladies that I frequently call or talk to. We just relate because we've been bouncing around, moving. We are just so used to moving around, so we relate on that.

Another noted,

> I think on a daily basis, because of the children, them going to school—and I put [other Army spouses] down for emergency contacts when I registered my children, I started developing a relationship with them. . . . And also just being a good neighbor and talking to [other spouses] in my neighborhood. And children's activities like girl scouts.

Army spouses we interviewed described their engagement with other spouses as mostly social in nature (rather than through formal groups such as SFRGs) and said that they considered other Army spouses their friends. Interview participants described interacting with other spouses both in person and online, noting the use of local installation Facebook spouse groups to engage with others both socially and for information about available resources.

Of the interview participants who noted little to no engagement with other Army spouses, many explained not having the desire to engage due to busy work schedules or other obligations in the civilian world; some noted cliquishness or gossiping among Army spouses that they did not wish to be a part of. One described her lack of engagement with other spouses:

> I work in a hospital in the civilian side, so that is where my exposure is. I am much more civilianized because I am not around a military setting often.

Another noted,

> I don't feel like I am connected with other Army spouses. Online they are rude, and in person there's a lot of drama. So I just stick to myself with my son.

As was noted in Chapter Three, interview participants frequently reported reaching out to other Army spouses for help with their problems. Notably, only about half of the participants who reported typically seeking assistance from other Army spouses also reported feeling connected to them. Although this comparison may not be representative of all spouses, the finding suggests that fostering connections may not be a prerequisite to achieve a sufficient connection to help them navigate the resource environment. For example, they can also get information from other spouses simply by reading posts made to Facebook pages.

Connections Through Solider and Family Readiness Groups

We also asked spouses about their engagement with SFRGs. Although few spouses had reported that they typically use SFRGs to find out about resources available to them, many participants reported being engaged with SFRGs to some degree, though the level of involvement varied. It ranged from serving in official SFRG roles, participating in in-person meetings, and engaging online to only receiving SFRG emails or connecting only on an as-needed basis. Most spouses who were engaged with SFRGs reported using them to get information about Army resources or answers to other Army-related questions. Some commented that they connected more with the SFRG when their active duty soldier was deployed. One spouse commented,

> I think FRG is a good program. They do a lot for family days. They typically have a good one. It's a good chance for face to face with other spouses. We almost had a deployment come up, and there was an information night come up with what to expect. That was nice. They were very friendly. They understand I am new and try to help me as much as possible.

Another noted,

> When my husband deployed I started being more involved. Every unit gets an FRG leader, and she gave me information about where my husband was and host[ed] social events. I went to a few of them, and that's how I meet other Army spouses.

Another commented on her SFRG engagement, which was online rather than in person:

> I'm connected via email. I don't do too much stuff because we are forty-five minutes away, so I don't do many in-person things. But I get information through email or on the Facebook page.

Respondents also noted that SFRGs can vary greatly in terms of quality and that the usefulness of a group is very dependent on the group's leadership.

Many interview participants reported that they had no SFRG engagement. Most of these spouses did not have a desire to connect with the SFRG, with some stating they did not need the resources or have the time to engage, and others noting the negative cliquish or gossipy aspects of SFRGs that they chose to avoid. One spouse commented,

> FRGs can be negative as well. They can be good to connect with other people in similar situations and the resources you need or opportunities coming up. But that's a healthy FRG—that's what it is meant to be. . . . But some FRGs are not great. Some are incredibly political and cliquish—there are some nasty arguments. And you don't know which kind of FRG you are getting when you show up at a new location. Here I entered into a whole bunch of drama that turned me off from those resources. It was also a huge time suck. I developed a distaste for the Army because of the FRG here.

Another stated,

> I am not connected with my FRG. The activities they have are more geared towards stay-at-home moms and those who don't work. A lot of the activities are during the day, when I work. I've been pretty much excluded from . . . everything.

A few spouses noted that they do not have active SFRGs at their active duty soldier's current assignment location, preventing their engagement. As one explained,

> We don't have an FRG here. A lot of the wives here didn't come with their husbands.

Another noted,

> I know there's supposed to be one. I was in communication with the FRG leader when we were in [another assignment location]. But I received nothing here. I never got anything like from there [the previous location] since I've been here.

Notably, those who reported no engagement with SFRGs were more likely to be the spouses of enlisted service members.

Helpfulness of Connections and Desire for Additional Connections

Even those who reported limited engagement stated that their connections with other Army spouses have been helpful to them. Participants noted that connections with other spouses were helpful for a range of reasons: as social connections, guides to military life and culture, sources of information about available resources or services, and useful entry points when arriving at a new location. One participant commented,

> I believe the best resource for Army spouses are other Army spouses. There is familiarity, and [it is] easier to speak to them about problems. It allows for quicker connections for people who have already gone through it.

Another noted,

> Yes, the [connections with other Army spouses] I do have have been helpful; especially spouses who have been married to someone a long time. They offer a lot of guidance surrounding benefits and things to do in the area.

Another spouse stated,

> [My connections with other Army spouses are] super helpful. Just the lifestyle we live, the [soldier] spouses don't work a nine-to-five job. It can be twenty-four hours or weeks or months for deployments. It's nice to have another spouse going through that. . . . I think that's been really helpful when you go through similar circumstances.

When asked if there were ways they would like to be more connected with other Army spouses, many interview participants stated that they did not desire any additional connections, often citing contentment with their current level of engagement, busy work schedules that did not allow additional time, or relationships with others (e.g., their active duty soldier, children, other family, or friends) that took up their time. One spouse commented,

> I'm not a hugely social person. I have a few good friends, and I'm satisfied.

Another described reasons for not desiring additional spouse connections:

> I own my own business and take care of a five-year-old, and that consumes most of my time.

Some interview participants who were asked about additional connections with other Army spouses reported a desire to be connected to a greater degree. Some of them wanted more social interaction with other spouses, including connecting with others who are parents to provide additional social outlets for their children. As one participant commented,

> More events, more spouses who want to be a part of things, like socializing. Socializing you can build up relationships to have connections, support each other as parents.

Another noted,

> I would like to have get-togethers with the kids or the children because my son is so young, and he is only around me. I would like him to have other interaction with other children.

Respondents also described a desire to be more connected with other spouses in order to be more informed about resources and other Army-related information. One spouse stated,

> I'd like to know more stuff. I'd like to know who runs the FRG, because I have no idea who to contact if my husband is in the field or another state. I know other people would like to know this too.

Interview participants who indicated a desire for more connections with other Army spouses tended to live close to installations, have children, and be married to enlisted members.

Connections with the Army Community Overall

Beyond connections with other Army spouses, we also asked interview participants to what degree they felt connected with the Army community overall. Many spouses interviewed indicated they did feel an overall connection. Notably, participants were more likely to report being connected with other Army spouses than with the Army community overall, and those spouses who reported differing levels of engagement with these two aspects of Army life were more likely to report connections with other Army spouses than with the Army community. Although these comparisons might not be representative of how all spouses think about the overall Army community, they suggest that connections with other spouses are particularly important for how respondents view the Army as a whole.

We probed the underlying reasons for a feeling of connection to the Army community. Many spouses who indicated they felt connected with the Army community said this was due to circumstance and proximity, such as being surrounded by neighbors who were in the Army or living in Army-friendly communities as opposed to larger, more urban areas. One spouse commented,

> We are very well connected [to the Army community]. You are surrounded by it all the time, so there is no moving away from it.

Another noted,

> There is a level of identity that I definitely feel as a result of Army life. If I tell people we are new to town, people assume we are military as a result.

Spouses also described participation in Army-sponsored events or resources and knowledge about Army culture as a means of feeling connected to the Army community. One spouse stated,

> I think [my connection to the Army community] is okay. . . . I know what some of the different bases and organizations do. I know what my husband does. I know what the organizations do, ACS, USO, and things like that. So, the commissary, the PX [post exchange], all those little kinds of things.

Some participants who reported little to no engagement with the Army community explained that it was due to their civilian work and social connections filling most of their time and being where they are most engaged. Some also mentioned not living on post or among other Army families, resulting in them not engaging in installation activities and the Army community. One spouse commented,

> I'm not very connected to the Army community right now. It's really about where we live. We aren't on post—it would be different if we were. We are kind of just in our own little enclave. We just aren't around other military families.

Another stated,

> I don't feel, overall, connected to the Army community. . . . I guess because my husband has been in a few years, and he's getting out, this is all super temporary. So, I don't feel like a big connection. I am older and have my own life and my own career. We also don't live on base. I make friends elsewhere. I don't have any sort of inkling to have a connection with Army people. If we were on base that was in the middle of nowhere, I am sure I would have a different attitude. This is a big town and a big city. You can really get what you want outside [the Army].

A few spouses noted negative experiences with members of the Army community that led to them feeling disconnected from it. One spouse commented,

> I don't feel connected at all. I feel like an outcast. When we go to things, I am often in the corner with my kids. I don't know what my husband does, I'm just kind of there.

Another mentioned,

> I don't feel connected with the Army community. Sometimes when we go out to the commissary or something, we would try to talk to people, but they don't talk to us.

We also asked interview participants if their connection to the Army community had varied over time and if, for example, their engagement with the Army at one garrison was stronger than at another. Of those spouses who had experienced multiple assignments, some said that their connections remained consistent over time, while most said that the degree to which they felt connected to the Army community had varied. Of those spouses who noted differences over time, some explained them as owing to the nature of their location. For example, spouses described being more connected with the Army community when living in a smaller area with more Army families as neighbors rather than in a larger urban area. One stated,

> It was different at our last location because our neighbors were all Army families. So, because they were our neighbors, we had a lot more connection with the Army community and Army families. Now we are just kind of by ourselves without that.

Some were more connected when their soldiers were stationed overseas; as one spouse explained,

> When we lived overseas, I had a lot more Army friends because I didn't have any civilian friends. . . . All our friends were military. After we left that very small environment, I've tried the coffees [with other Army spouses], but it does not interest me.

Some spouses attributed the variation in Army community engagement they experienced to personal circumstances that changed over time, such as putting down roots in an area, parental status, children's age, or employment status, as well as just differences in connecting or "clicking" with individuals at various installations. For example, one spouse noted,

> [My connection to the Army community] is stronger here. Honestly, it's because we bought a house here and I care to make those connections. I was too busy before to connect to people. I tend to be the best at what I am doing, and that includes relationships and friendships. If I have too much going on, I won't add to that.

Another commented,

> I would say it was stronger at other places. I don't think it has to do with anything that the military is involved with. We just sometimes click with some people. There are certain men that my husband's gotten along with, and when we hang out, and there's a connection between the spouses, then we hang out. Doesn't matter how far we live from each other, or how often we work, we can still find time. I don't think it's anything that the military does. Some people connect and some people don't.

Another mentioned that social media becoming more prevalent had contributed to her becoming more connected over time:

> Yeah, in the beginning, like in our first duty station, Facebook wasn't as big. There weren't those pages as features available. So, I had to find those things on my own. But now I am better connected with social media.

Summary

In terms of outcomes reported on the TASS, Fort Carson spouses reported more stress and fewer positive attitudes toward the military, though given that they were very similar to spouses elsewhere with regard to the problems they reported and aspects of the problem-solving process, it seems unlikely that the nature of their problems or ability to find help is the cause of those differences. Compared with the overall averages, spouses at Fort Benning reported more positive attitudes toward the military and a greater level of social support from their military network. With these exceptions, however, differences in the aspects we examined tended *not* to form a pattern that might suggest systemic differences in the experience of Army spouses across garrisons.

Although the interviews are not meant to be representative of the perceptions or experiences of all Army spouses, they provide a more in-depth exploration of their connections with other spouses as well as with the Army community overall. Most participants reported feeling engaged with other Army spouses, and those who reported feeling engaged described interacting with other spouses both in person and online, noting the use of local installations' Facebook spouse groups. Of those not engaged with other spouses, they attributed this to busy work schedules or other obligations, as well as a cliquishness or gossiping among Army spouses that they did not wish to be a part of.

Given the role of SFRG as a mechanism to involve Army spouses in the goings-on of the unit and the potential of this avenue to help foster connections between Army spouses, we explored spouses' engagement with this program. In terms of engagement with SFRGs specifically, about half of interview participants reported being engaged with SFRGs to some degree, though the level of involvement ranged from serving in official SFRG roles to only receiving SFRG emails or connecting only on an as-needed basis. Those who reported no engagement with SFRGs were more likely to be the spouses of enlisted service members. Interview participants noted that the quality and usefulness of SFRGs can vary significantly by location and be dependent on group leadership. Interview participants noted that even if they had limited engagement with other Army spouses, these connections have been helpful to them. However, many participants stated they did not desire additional connections with other spouses and were content with their current level of engagement.

Most spouses interviewed noted minimal or no connection with the Army overall, and they were more likely to report being connected with other Army spouses than with the Army community. Proximity to other Army families and the local installation, as well as civilian life obligations, were reported to affect participants' engagement levels. Most interview participants described their connections with the Army community as varying over time, often dependent on the nature of the location of the assignment, such as whether they were located in a large urban area versus a small community with other Army families.

CHAPTER SIX

Conclusions and Recommendations

This report has used previously collected survey data and recent qualitative interviews with Army spouses to explore their experiences with navigating the military and nonmilitary resource landscape to find the help they need. We particularly focused on the connections that Army spouses form with each other and with the Army community as a whole and how those connections might constitute gateways to foster better resource navigation and more effective resource use, although we do not assess the use or effectiveness of these resources for helping spouses solve their problems.

Project Strengths and Limitations

As with all research, some caveats bear mention, though our mixed-methods approach helps balance some of the caveats that come with each individual method, qualitative or quantitative. Our quantitative approach has a primary advantage of being able to ensure that, within the limitations of sampling and response, our results are representative of the targeted population of Army spouses. Moreover, our targeted and branching survey questions do offer a closer look at the process of problem solving (in a standardized manner), than might otherwise be found with a set of common questions (although they cannot speak to the detail of individual experiences). However, the survey was not originally designed to acquire a large, representative sample of spouses *at all Army garrisons* (e.g., the project did not sample more spouses from smaller garrisons to increase representation of those locations). The garrisons analyzed in this report were only those that had enough respondents to reasonably be included in the analysis and are not meant to be representative of all CONUS Army garrisons or specific types of garrisons. As suggested in our interview results, Army spouses who live overseas may have different needs and access to resources than those living in the United States, and future research should examine the problem-solving processes among these spouses.

Qualitative work such as our interviews helps fill in some gaps in quantitative data, especially in terms of enabling us to probe deeply into the detail of individual experiences. Similar to our survey methodology, however, our interviews are subject to unique limitations. Although we tried to attain diversity within our sample, we spoke in depth with only about 40 spouses, too few to be representative of the larger population of Army spouses. Their experiences are their own. However, we were able to explore in depth how those spouses experienced the resource landscape provided by the Army and how their experiences with problem solving as a process occurred. We were also able to explore in more depth the influence of community on that process.

The majority of the data presented, both quantitative (survey) and qualitative (interviews), reflects individual perceptions. Thus, the data are uniquely suited to offer insights into how Army spouses perceive and cope with the problem-solving process and what resources they perceive are available. Particularly when considering the interview suggestions regarding improvements to services, it is important to note that these are the perceptions of the customer base of those services. Service providers may have a different view of availability and customer service, as well as a greater awareness of funding limitations that preclude implementing some of the proffered suggestions. However, awareness of perceptions of the actual customer base—Army spouses and their families, including soldiers—provides needed insights into how people find and navigate Army programs and services.

It is important to note that most of the qualitative interviews were conducted before the COVID-19 pandemic disrupted military and civilian life (i.e., before mid-March 2020). The shutdowns of schools and military childcare, as well as potential delays in PCS moves and loss of employment for spouses, could have created major problems that spouses needed to address. In addition, if interviews had been conducted during the pandemic, physical distancing restrictions could have affected spouses' perceptions of the Army community and their suggestions for improvements (e.g., for in-person welcome sessions). At this point it is unclear how much of a long-term impact the pandemic will have on Army family life, but we note that it did not have an impact on the results of this project. We conducted few interviews during the pandemic, and interview participants were asked about problems they experienced in the past year—typical experiences finding resources and the like. Thus, their responses were not affected by temporary restrictions or shutdowns during the height of the pandemic. In addition, no interview participants mentioned the pandemic or related issues in any of their responses. We reasoned that the issues facing interview and survey participants are likely to continue regardless of the pandemic—for example, spouses will likely continue to have difficulty navigating the military resource system—and some existing issues are likely to be amplified because of the pandemic, such as the experience of loneliness and the need for connection to others in the Army community. Thus, we conclude that our main findings will continue to be valid in the postpandemic world, but we have modified our recommendations somewhat to address potential changes to the status quo (e.g., in-person welcome sessions were desired by spouses, but they may not be feasible if physical distancing restrictions continue to be needed).

Despite these caveats, we judge that our approach has achieved the aims of balancing quantitative advantages with qualitative ones; explored more deeply how Army spouses navigate the resource system and engage the military community to find the help they need; and noted whether that navigation varies across garrisons. Moreover, we think the mixed-methods approach provides a set of useful and interesting findings. We turn now to these findings.

Summary of Key Findings

We analyzed the survey data through the lens of spouses' experiences at different CONUS garrisons, reasoning that the problem-solving process might vary across garrisons due to differences in geographic or site-specific conditions. *However, rather than differences, our primary finding is the universality of experience: commonalities across garrisons in the problems spouses experienced, their needs for help with their problems, the resources used to help meet those needs, and whether their needs were met by those resources.*

There were a few potential exceptions. One was the number and type of problems experienced by spouses at JBLM; spouses at this garrison experienced more problems than average and were more likely to prioritize health care system problems. JBLM spouses also reported fewer positive attitudes toward the military than did spouses at other locations. In terms of outcomes, Fort Carson spouses reported more stress and fewer positive attitudes toward the military, though, given that they were very similar to those of spouses elsewhere with regard to the problems they reported and aspects of the problem-solving process, the nature of their problems or spouses' ability to get help with their problems seems unlikely to be the cause of those differences. In contrast, *spouses at Fort Benning experienced more positive outcomes than average and reported higher levels of social support from their military network and more positive attitudes toward the military.* It is possible that Fort Benning could offer clues to potential gateways to better integrate spouses into the Army community. The Army could consider investigating the aspects of family life at Fort Benning that encourage a greater sense of community—that is, if there are stable conditions at this garrison that encourage stronger community connections or offer an expanded network of influential "weak ties" and whether these conditions might offer lessons for ways to increase spouses' sense of community at other garrisons.

With these exceptions, however, differences in the aspects we examined tended *not* to form a pattern that might suggest systemic differences in the experience of Army spouses navigating the resource landscape. This suggests that, on the whole, interventions can take an Army-wide approach, though some challenges that spouses are likely to face are inherently more local (e.g., employment).

Our interviews expanded on prior survey findings that spouses contacted over four resources when seeking help for their most pressing problems (Trail, Sims, and Tankard, 2019). Interview data address the *experience of successful referrals to more appropriate resources for their problems*, as well as the *experience of getting "bounced around" and the challenges in resource navigation that they (as well as their soldiers) may experience.* Our survey findings indicate that solicitation of multiple resources for help in solving problems is common regardless of location. And, regardless of location, some needs go unmet. Interviewed spouses related stories of being successfully referred to another, more appropriate resource when one was unable to assist, but they also reported seeking additional help on their own when they hit a dead end with one resource that was unable to help them and they had to start over in their search for resources. The latter experiences suggest that warm handoffs among resources were not always the norm.

Although the number of resources and complexity of process were not characteristic of a given problem domain, many spouses who reported using multiple resources had Army-specific problems. Notably, when asked what would improve resources, spouses spoke of how a "one-stop shop" would be helpful. This suggests some unfamiliarity with the intent of ACS and Military OneSource to serve as one-stop shops. However, when asked about their process in solving problems, some spouses did note that those resources served the function of providing an entryway that helped them locate what they needed to resolve their challenges. The resources mentioned most often in the interviews, however, were other Army spouses—via social media or in person.

We queried interviewees regarding the types of engagement they appreciated. Building on previous survey findings for spouses' preferred modes of contact (Trail, Sims, and Tankard, 2019), *interviewees appreciated multiple modalities of contact*, with some mentioning that they felt comfortable engaging over social media, some noting pamphlets distributed on garrison to highlight available resources, and some explaining that they used SFRGs as a source of information about resources. Interview participants most often reported that they received information about resources from other Army spouses, again echoing the previous survey findings (Trail, Sims, and Tankard, 2019). This is also a common finding across garrisons, with the second most common resource cited by spouses being other Army spouses, for 12 out of 13 locations.

When asked how best to improve connections to resources, several spouses suggested providing comprehensive welcome sessions or information packets when they arrive at a new installation—another "high-touch" solution. Spouses also cited the need for a centralized repository for local installation resources—preferably a website with all the resources in one place. This suggests that they either do not use Military OneSource—which is designed to serve this function—in the manner intended or that they want the centralized website to include more than just military resources.

When asked about *perceived reputations of various resources, interviewees noted that housing and health care services were perceived as having negative reputations.* Although for the most part neither problem area was prominently reported in the survey, reports of health care system problems were significantly more frequent at JBLM, as noted previously. More encouraging is some interviewees reporting that they perceived no Army program as having a negative reputation. When asked about programs perceived as having a positive reputation, interviewees reported finding ACS and MWR to be helpful, suggesting that those programs could serve as gateways to other programs for spouses. Indeed, that is explicitly part of ACS's mission.

Interview participants noted that *connections with other spouses were helpful for a range of reasons:* as social connections, guides to military life and culture, sources of information about available resources or services, and useful entry points when arriving at a new location. We used the interviews, in particular, to explore Army spouses' experiences of forming such connections. Most spouses interviewed reported contentment with their level of connection and did not desire a closer one. In terms of *already* feeling connected, spouses described their connection to other Army spouses as mostly social in nature rather than through formal groups such as SFRGs, and that they considered other Army spouses their friends. Of those spouses who reported feeling engaged, they noted commonalities that led to this feeling, often relating to connections due to children or proximity but also describing connecting to spouses online through social media.

In addition to proximity and commonalities, interview participants reported that the obligations of civilian life affected their level of engagement with the Army community; some reported being too busy with other commitments (including civilian employment) to want or need a higher level of engagement. Moreover, many interview participants reported that their connection varied over time and context. For example, living in smaller communities or communities with a higher concentration of Army families resulted in closer ties, as did life course events such as having children, which encouraged them to make use of available Army resources. Despite this natural ebb and flow, *Army resources and, more generally, social contact with the Army community is something that offers spouses and their soldiers opportunities to alleviate the challenges of military life and which the Army has reason to facilitate for families in need.*

Recommendations

Our findings suggest that, for the most part, challenges facing spouses and their experiences navigating the resource landscape are common across the Army. As with the general resources provided (ACS, Child and Youth Services, MWR, and others), this suggests that a common Army approach implemented locally produces relatively similar results across CONUS garrisons and is a reasonable approach to take.

As is clear from our previous work (Sims, Trail, Chen, Miller, Meza, et al., 2018; Trail, Sims, and Tankard, 2019) and from the interviews conducted for the current project, spouses need a gateway through which to avail themselves of the benefits of being part of the Army community. This is especially true of spouses who are young and new to the military (i.e., spouses of junior enlisted soldiers), but even those with more military experience can have new situations that require connecting to the community to get information and resources. Furthermore, the expansive literature on social support demonstrates the positive benefit of additional instrumental, informational, and emotional support for coping with challenges (see, e.g., Cohen and Wills, 1985; Taylor, 2011), and even occasional or peripheral connections to a community can provide informational support to community members through the provision of novel information and resources (Chewning and Montemurro, 2016; Granovetter, 1984). There are a number of formal and informal ways spouses can form a gateway to the Army community, and the bulk of our recommendations are designed to expand those gateways or enhance the current ones.

One prominent and often informal gateway to the Army community is other Army spouses, who were cited by respondents as one of the most frequently accessed resources

(Trail, Sims, and Tankard, 2019). Most interviewees reported that their connections with other spouses were very useful in either directly providing help for a problem or directing them to resources to help them meet their needs. Interviews revealed that most spouses experienced different levels of connection to the Army community depending on where their soldiers were garrisoned.

Although the Army has little direct control over whether spouses form informal relationships with each other, SFRGs are one formal way to connect them with one another and to the Army community, and a greater focus by SFRGs on connecting spouses to each other could foster greater informal social relationships. Although SFRGs are explicitly tasked with connecting spouses (and soldiers) to resources and to each other, negative perceptions of SFRGs persist among some spouses. Echoing prior survey research (Trail, Sims, and Tankard, 2019), interview participants did not often note SFRGs as a source of help for challenges, and spouses in our interviews reported the same types of concerns with this resource as have been found in prior work (Sims, Trail, Chen, Miller, Meza, et al., 2018). However, SFRGs serve a potentially useful social support function in the sense that they are uniquely positioned to help Army spouses engage with each other and hence to serve as a gateway to the Army community. Moreover, the most frequent need cited by survey respondents was for emotional and social support (Trail, Sims, and Tankard, 2019), and SFRGs are one Army-controlled resource that is best positioned to provide that support to spouses. Though interviewees did not report SFRGs as a resource for getting help with their issues, many did nonetheless report that they were engaged with an SFRG at least tangentially. Finally, to the extent that SFRGs serve as a gateway to connection with other Army spouses, they have utility for helping spouses resolve the problems they experience, as other Army spouses and word of mouth were preferred by interviewees, as well as, more generally, survey respondents (see Trail, Sims, and Tankard, 2019). Thus, **SFRGs should be specifically leveraged as a means to inform spouses of what is available and should continue to provide a venue for connection with the Army community when such a connection is desired**. This can be done directly through SFRG activities, such as incorporating organized spouse activities beyond SFRG meetings, such as sports or games, but also by introducing (or reintroducing) SFRGs to spouses through other formal or informal activities. When possible, these activities should be conducted in person, but interactive online activities could also be incorporated into SFRGs (e.g., games, moderated forums, and the like).

One way the Army can introduce spouses to SFRGs and other gateways to the Army community is by **conducting strategically planned welcome sessions—ideally, in person—just for spouses who recently experienced a PCS to a garrison**. These sessions would not only serve as a potential gateway to the available resources themselves (through the provision of information about the garrison and local Army and civilian resources) but would also offer a venue whereby spouses new to the garrison might be able to connect with other similarly situated spouses. Some locations are already doing this, but a more systematic approach may prove helpful to the Army. For example, the Army could explore using specific activities to strategically encourage these connections, such as by **introducing a spouse mentor or buddy**

system that is organized and centralized at the garrison after PCS moves that allows each new spouse to be connected with a matched spouse who is already established and active in the Army community. Furthermore, **spouse email addresses could be gathered at the session and incorporated into a garrison-specific listserv.** Almost half of Army spouses indicated that they wanted to be contacted with information about Army resources via email (Trail, Sims, and Tankard, 2019), and gathering email addresses at a welcome session is one way to establish an email list. When provided, these sessions should be scheduled at a time and location that is convenient for spouses.

However, such an in-person gathering would not be sufficient to provide spouses with all the information they need about the resources available to them, especially given their different preferences for connection to other spouses and their preferred mode of connection (i.e., in person or online). **A webpage where spouses can follow-up on resources provided during the initial in-person session might also prove useful.** Spouses may not need the flood of information presented at such gatherings until they are faced with a problem, and having such a convenient resource would facilitate the ongoing usefulness of the sessions for the duration of their tenure at a given garrison.

In addition, welcome sessions and SFRG gateways to the Army community could be supplemented by other formal, interactive online activities providing connection and social support to Army spouses. We suggest that the Army **incorporate moderated online forums specifically for spouses seeking help.** Respondents reported reaching out to other spouses through informal Facebook spouse groups, and previously reported survey results suggest that Facebook is one of the most preferred gateways for spouses to get information about the resources available to meet their needs (Trail, Sims, and Tankard, 2019). Spouses could be directed to the moderated forum through a listserv and through outreach to the existing informal Facebook spouse groups. A more formal online gateway that still provides interactive help could be one way to reach spouses who live far from post and want greater connections to the Army community, but it could also be a gateway for better access to occasional as-needed connections for spouses who reported that they did not want to directly connect with other spouses because they perceive them as unwelcoming, gossipy, or cliquey. A moderator would exert greater control over those less welcoming aspects of online forums and provide greater support for spouses who need help and an alternative online gateway to the Army community.

Finally, interviews reinforced previous survey findings suggesting that even spouses who are relatively connected to the Army community sometimes have difficulty accessing and navigating the Army system (Trail, Sims, and Tankard, 2019). The interviews offered insight into the difficulties spouses had finding information about garrison resources and suggested that a more accessible online presence of military resources that is consistent across garrisons would help spouses navigate the military system. Although resources are local, **more prominence of Military OneSource as a guide to finding *local* resources—both military and civilian—and more clarity regarding the possibility of using that website for such a purpose may be helpful.** As it is, navigating the site to find local resources can be intimidating. Moreover, **more consistency across garrison homepages with regard to information regarding services** might also help spouses find resources. Across websites there should be an emphasis on ease of access for spouses (e.g., a webpage that does not require a common access card), frequent updates so that the information is current, and general user-friendliness to help spouses quickly and efficiently find the information they need. Google was another frequently noted resource, and it could obviate difficulties navigating garrison homepages. However, it is unclear whether Army or other military resources have optimized their likelihood of coming up as "hits" for particular types of searches. **As a sophisticated service provider, it behooves the Army to make sure Army spouses using Google or other search engines to search for resources are likely to be connected with appropriate Army resources**.

Many of the interviewees who reported seeking multiple resources did so when the first was unable to help or otherwise did not help. Spouses may find other resources themselves, or their initial service provider may refer them to another resource that is believed to be more appropriate for a given problem. As noted in previous work (Sims, Trail, Chen, Miller, Meza, et al., 2018; Trail, Sims, and Tankard, 2019), Army programs and leadership should establish a "no wrong door" policy through which spouses who contact them for help can be directed to the most appropriate resource for their problem, even if that resource falls outside the purview of the program or leader. Part of this policy should be to train leaders and program staff on the resources available to Army families and how best to refer family members to those resources (Sims, Trail, Chen, Miller, Meza, et al., 2018). For these referrals, a best practice in health care is that the referring provider directly connect a spouse with the referred resource—that is, a warm handoff. It is unclear from the interviews or survey data whether warm handoffs in family programs are the norm, but it is clear that some spouses had to seek other resources on their own without the benefit of a warm handoff. **As a best practice, warm handoffs between programs should be the standard rather than the exception**, particularly since our interviewees suggest that the need for such transfers is greatest for Army-specific problems such as PCS moves.

Although the Army offers a wide variety of resources to help military families solve Army-related challenges and day-to-day challenges such as child care, survey results and discussions with Army spouses suggest that it is not always easy to find these resources when they are needed. In turn, some families are not able to get the help they need. Not all spouses desire greater connection with the Army community, but the research literature and Army spouses themselves point to the utility of such connections, as social support serves a useful function for resolving life's troubles. The Army should take steps to further the ability of Army spouses to increase connections with each other and the rest of the Army community when they desire to, and to make it easier for all spouses to get information on available resources and identify the resources appropriate to their needs. Our recommendations suggest specific actions the Army could pursue.

Additional Survey Data Results

This appendix provides additional detail on subgroup differences in the loneliness and social support outcomes reported in Chapter Five. It also includes tables detailing nonmilitary resource use by spouses at different garrisons, as discussed in Chapter Three.

Subgroup Differences in Spouse Outcomes

Since the analysis of spouses' reports of loneliness or social support did not appear in the earlier report detailing TASS results (Trail, Sims, and Tankard, 2019), we detail significant subgroup differences on those variables here (using a criterion p-value of .01 or less). As was noted in Chapter Two, we included the following sociodemographic characteristics as covariates in our multiple regression models: the spouse's employment status, the presence of dependent children in the household, housing location, the soldier's pay grade, and whether the soldier deployed in the past year.

Spouses' reports of loneliness significantly differed according to their own employment statuses and their soldiers' pay grades. Spouses who were unemployed and looking for work reported significantly higher levels of loneliness (mean = 2.87, 99-percent CI: 2.78 to 2.96) than did spouses employed full-time (mean = 2.68, 99-percent CI: 2.62 to 2.75) and spouses who were unemployed and not looking for work (mean = 2.74, 99-percent CI: 2.68 to 2.79), but they did not significantly differ from spouses employed part-time (mean = 2.75, 99-percent CI: 2.66 to 2.84). Among pay grade groups, spouses of junior enlisted soldiers reported significantly higher levels of loneliness (mean = 2.85, 99-percent CI: 2.78 to 2.93) than did spouses of all other pay grade groups (senior enlisted mean = 2.72, 99-percent CI: 2.67 to 2.77; junior officers mean = 2.65, 99-percent CI: 2.57 to 2.73; and senior officers mean = 2.66, 99-percent CI: 2.57 to 2.75). No other significant differences emerged for spouses' reported levels of loneliness.

Examining subgroup differences in spouses' levels of support from their informal military social networks (i.e., military-connected family and friends), significant differences emerged for distance from post and soldier's pay grade. We found a significant trend in that the farther spouses lived from post, the less support they reported receiving from their informal military social networks. For pay grade, spouses of junior enlisted soldiers reported lower levels of support from their informal military social networks (mean = 3.04, 99-percent CI: 2.95 to 3.12) than did spouses of senior enlisted soldiers (mean = 3.16, 99-percent CI: 3.11 to 3.21). Spouses of both junior and senior enlisted soldiers reported lower levels of support from their informal military social networks than did spouses of junior officers (mean = 3.52, 99-percent CI: 3.43 to 3.61) and spouses of senior officers (mean = 3.50, 99-percent CI: 3.40 to 3.59). No other significant differences emerged from the analysis.

Finally, spouses' reports of levels of support from their informal social networks outside the military significantly differed according to their own employment statuses, the presence of dependent children in the household, and soldiers' pay grades. Spouses who were unemployed and looking for work reported significantly less support from their social networks outside the military (mean = 3.74, 99-percent CI: 3.65 to 3.83) than did spouses employed full-time (mean =3.88, 99-percent CI: 3.81 to 3.94), part-time (mean = 3.90, 99-percent CI: 3.81 to 3.98), and spouses who were unemployed and not looking for work (mean = 3.91, 99-percent CI: 3.86 to 3.96). Spouses with children reported less support from their social networks outside the military (mean = 3.85, 99-percent CI: 3.81 to 3.89) than did spouses without children (mean = 3.93, 99-percent CI: 3.87 to 4.00). Spouses of junior officers reported significantly more support from their social networks outside the military (mean = 4.06, 99-percent CI: 3.98 to 4.13) than did spouses of junior enlisted (mean = 3.82, 99-percent CI: 3.75 to 3.90) or senior enlisted soldiers (mean = 3.85, 99-percent CI: 3.81 to 3.90). Spouses of senior officers reported significantly more support from their social networks outside the military (mean = 3.95, 99-percent CI: 3.87 to 4.04) than did spouses of junior enlisted soldiers. No other significant differences emerged from the analysis.

Spouse Use of Nonmilitary Resources by Garrison

Tables A.1 and A.2 display the nonmilitary resources included in the survey, along with the percentage of respondents who indicated that they accessed each resource to address their needs (respondents could choose more than one resource for each problem-need pair). As was reported in Chapter Three, there were no significant differences in nonmilitary resource use among spouses at different garrisons.

TABLE A.1

Percentage of Respondents and 99-Percent Confidence Intervals for Nonmilitary Resources Used to Address Needs, by Garrison

	Government Resources for Family Services	Private Clubs, Organizations, Recreation Centers	Private Off-Post Childcare	Religious or Spiritual Groups or Leaders	Private Mental Health Care Providers	Private Medical Providers	Government Resources for Family Services
Army average	15.0	19.5	11.0	19.8	11.2	12.8	35.2
Fort Benning	15.6 (9.6, 21.6)	23.4 (16.7, 30.2)	13.7 (8.1, 19.3)	20.5 (14.1, 26.8)	16.5 (10.4, 22.6)	11.1 (6.1, 16.0)	39.3 (31.5, 47.1)
Fort Bliss	14.2 (9.7, 18.7)	16.3 (11.6, 21.0)	11.0 (7.0, 15.0)	22.2 (17.0, 27.5)	11.7 (7.6, 15.8)	12.6 (8.3, 16.9)	33.2 (27.1, 39.2)
Fort Bragg	13.1 (9.8, 16.4)	19.2 (15.5, 22.9)	11.8 (8.7, 14.9)	18.4 (14.8, 22.1)	10.4 (7.5, 13.3)	12.6 (9.5, 15.8)	34.6 (30.0, 39.1)
Fort Campbell	15.5 (11.0, 20.1)	18.7 (13.8, 23.6)	9.2 (5.6, 12.7)	24.9 (19.5, 30.3)	9.4 (5.8, 13.0)	9.8 (6.1, 13.5)	33.2 (27.3, 39.1)
Fort Carson	12.6 (8.0, 17.1)	18.3 (13.2, 23.5)	10.4 (6.4, 14.5)	20.5 (15.2, 25.9)	14.2 (9.6, 18.9)	14.3 (9.6, 19.0)	35.8 (29.3, 42.3)
Fort Drum	20.7 (13.6, 27.8)	18.3 (11.7, 24.8)	9.0 (4.3, 13.7)	19.4 (12.7, 26.1)	9.9 (4.8, 14.9)	12.8 (6.9, 18.6)	37.9 (29.6, 46.3)
Fort Gordon	15.6 (8.2, 23.1)	20.5 (12.5, 28.5)	9.3 (3.7, 14.9)	17.8 (10.3, 25.2)	9.6 (3.8, 15.5)	13.4 (6.7, 20.0)	41.7 (31.9, 51.6)
Fort Hood	17.4 (12.7, 22.1)	19.5 (14.8, 24.2)	11.0 (7.3, 14.7)	21.3 (16.5, 26.2)	12.0 (8.1, 16.0)	14.0 (9.8, 18.2)	33.1 (27.5, 38.8)
Fort Leonard Wood	13.0 (5.4, 20.5)	17.8 (9.6, 26.1)	10.0 (3.6, 16.4)	21.8 (12.8, 30.8)	6.2 (0.9, 11.5)	9.4 (2.8, 15.9)	32.3 (22.1, 42.5)
Fort Riley	16.8 (10.8, 22.7)	20.3 (14.1, 26.6)	14.2 (8.7, 19.6)	20.0 (13.7, 26.2)	12.1 (6.9, 17.3)	12.5 (7.3, 17.7)	34.0 (26.5, 41.6)
Fort Sill	17.4 (8.2, 26.6)	16.3 (8.0, 24.7)	6.4 (0.6, 12.2)	14.5 (6.6, 22.5)	11.1 (3.5, 18.8)	11.7 (4.0, 19.4)	27.4 (17.0, 37.8)
Fort Stewart	16.1 (10.4, 21.9)	20.3 (14.3, 26.3)	10.0 (5.4, 14.5)	18.4 (12.6, 24.2)	9.1 (4.6, 13.5)	9.4 (5.0, 13.9)	34.4 (27.1, 41.7)
JBLM	15.1 (10.6, 19.6)	24.0 (18.8, 29.2)	13.2 (9.2, 17.2)	19.1 (14.3, 23.9)	11.9 (7.9, 15.9)	16.3 (11.7, 20.8)	37.2 (31.2, 43.2)
Other garrisons	14.1 (11.4, 16.7)	19.3 (16.4, 22.2)	10.8 (8.5, 13.0)	17.8 (15.0, 20.6)	10.8 (8.5, 13.1)	13.4 (10.8, 15.9)	36.4 (32.8, 40.0)

NOTES: N = 5,826. Percentages are within garrison for respondents who reported problems, needs, and used resources. Since respondents could list up to two needs for each of their two prioritized problems, percentages may add up to more than 100 percent. CIs help convey the uncertainty that is found in any estimate; for the 99-percent CIs that we report, if we measured the same variables in the same way from the same population, in 99 percent of those samples our results would fall within the upper and lower bounds that we report.

TABLE A.2

Percentage of Respondents and 99-Percent Confidence Intervals for Nonmilitary Resources Used to Address Needs, by Garrison

	Internet Resources	Unofficial Social Media Military Networks	Other Military Spouses You Know in Person	Personal Networks Outside the Military	Civilian Employers	Nonmilitary Contacts
Army average	35.2	27.9	42.5	52.0	9.5	8.3
Fort Benning	39.3 (31.5, 47.1)	32.0 (24.6, 39.5)	44.1 (36.1, 52.0)	52.4 (44.3, 60.4)	7.2 (3.0, 11.4)	6.5 (2.6, 10.3)
Fort Bliss	33.2 (27.1, 39.2)	23.8 (18.3, 29.2)	43.5 (37.2, 49.8)	53.6 (47.2, 60.0)	9.1 (5.3, 12.8)	9.0 (5.5, 12.6)
Fort Bragg	34.6 (30.0, 39.1)	25.3 (21.2, 29.5)	45.4 (40.7, 50.2)	55.1 (50.4, 59.9)	9.3 (6.5, 12.1)	8.3 (5.8, 10.9)
Fort Campbell	33.2 (27.3, 39.1)	28.7 (23.1, 34.4)	44.1 (37.9, 50.4)	53.2 (46.9, 59.5)	8.6 (5.0, 12.2)	7.0 (3.8, 10.2)
Fort Carson	35.8 (29.3, 42.3)	28.2 (22.1, 34.3)	40.6 (34.0, 47.2)	52.2 (45.5, 58.9)	10.2 (6.1, 14.4)	5.2 (2.3, 8.0)
Fort Drum	37.9 (29.6, 46.3)	35.3 (27.1, 43.5)	43.9 (35.4, 52.4)	52.4 (43.8, 61.0)	11.2 (5.8, 16.6)	8.0 (3.4, 12.6)
Fort Gordon	41.7 (31.9, 51.6)	29.5 (20.4, 38.5)	41.3 (31.5, 51.1)	52.8 (42.9, 62.7)	11.1 (4.9, 17.3)	7.7 (2.3, 13.1)
Fort Hood	33.1 (27.5, 38.8)	26.4 (21.1, 31.6)	41.8 (35.9, 47.7)	48.4 (42.4, 54.4)	10.0 (6.5, 13.6)	8.4 (5.1, 11.7)
Fort Leonard Wood	32.3 (22.1, 42.5)	26.0 (16.4, 35.5)	41.2 (30.5, 51.9)	51.3 (40.4, 62.2)	9.9 (3.4, 16.4)	9.0 (2.7, 15.3)
Fort Riley	34.0 (26.5, 41.6)	32.0 (24.6, 39.4)	46.6 (38.7, 54.5)	56.8 (49.0, 64.7)	11.9 (6.7, 17.2)	6.1 (2.4, 9.8)
Fort Sill	27.4 (17.0, 37.8)	25.5 (15.3, 35.6)	42.5 (31.1, 54.0)	42.8 (31.3, 54.3)	12.3 (4.2, 20.4)	7.7 (1.9, 13.6)
Fort Stewart	34.4 (27.1, 41.7)	28.1 (21.2, 34.9)	40.6 (33.1, 48.1)	46.8 (39.1, 54.5)	9.5 (5.1, 13.9)	6.8 (3.1, 10.5)
JBLM	37.2 (31.2, 43.2)	27.8 (22.3, 33.3)	40.6 (34.5, 46.6)	56.2 (50.0, 62.3)	10.5 (6.7, 14.3)	7.9 (4.6, 11.3)
Other garrisons	36.4 (32.8, 40.0)	28.3 (25.0, 31.7)	40.7 (37.1, 44.3)	49.5 (45.8, 53.2)	8.0 (6.0, 10.0)	11.0 (8.7, 13.3)

NOTES: $N = 5,826$. Percentages are within garrison for respondents who reported problems, needs, and used resources. Since respondents could list up to two needs for each of their two prioritized problems, percentages may add up to more than 100 percent. CIs help convey the uncertainty that is found in any estimate; for the 99-percent CIs that we report, if we measured the same variables in the same way from the same population, in 99 percent of those samples our results would fall within the upper and lower bounds that we report.

Army Spouse Invitation, Informed Consent, and Interview Protocol

Email Invitation for Participation

Hello,

You may remember that, when you completed the Today's Army Spouse Survey in 2018, you indicated that you were interested in participating in future research projects through RAND, an independent, nonprofit, research institution. We have one such opportunity for you! We are doing a study for the Army that delves more deeply into how Army spouses find and navigate Army and civilian resources to help them cope with challenges.

As part of this study, we are interviewing a small set of people who responded to the survey. This would be a phone interview where we call you to discuss your experiences with Army programs and services and your perceptions of those programs and services. The interview will take about 30 minutes, and we will give you a $20 Amazon.com gift card as a token of our appreciation for your help.

If you are interested in participating in a phone interview and your spouse is still in the Army, just respond to this email and we will get back to you to set up a time to talk.

Thank you for considering this opportunity. We look forward to hearing back from you!

Regards,
Today's Army Spouse Survey Team
RAND Corporation

Informed Consent

Project Title: Assessing the Needs of Army Families: Spouse Perspectives
Principal Investigators: Carra Sims and Thomas Trail

You are being invited to participate in a research study. We are interested in learning about how you and your family find and navigate Army and civilian resources when you need them. We will be asking you a series of questions about your experiences with Army programs and services and your perceptions of those programs and services.

Your participation is completely voluntary and you are under no obligation to discuss anything that you do not feel comfortable discussing with us. We will keep all information you provide during the discussion confidential. You may refuse to answer any questions that you do not want to answer and still remain in the study. Refusal to answer questions will not have any negative consequences, and you will still be compensated with a $20 gift card from Amazon.com.

Your name and contact information will be kept completely separate from your responses, and we will not share the names of our interview participants with anyone outside the RAND study team. The information you provide will help us understand people's experiences finding and navigating Army and civilian resources and how these resources have or have not helped you. The information you provide will be combined with that collected from other interviews and presented collectively in a final report that we will present to the Army and release publicly.

We will be taking notes on the call to ensure that we accurately capture your comments, but we will not identify you by name in these notes nor in our final report. The notes will be seen only by those at RAND working on the project and they will be destroyed following the completion of the report.

This study is sponsored by the Army Soldier and Family Readiness Division within the Office of the Deputy Chief of Staff, G-9.

If you have questions about your rights as a research participant or need to report a research-related injury or concern, you can contact RAND's Human Subjects Protection Committee toll-free at (868) 697-5620 or by emailing hspcinfo@rand.org. When you contact the committee, please reference Study 2018-0799.

Army Spouse Interview Protocol

Background Questions

1. To confirm, are you currently married to an active duty Army soldier? What is your spouse's rank?

2. What is your military status (e.g., currently in the active duty military, currently in the Reserves or National Guard, not currently serving in the military)?

3. Where of the following best describes where you live? (*If you have PCS'd or moved locally in the past year, please answer with respect to the place where you were located for more than half the time.*)
   a. Privatized military housing on post
   b. Military family housing on post
   c. Military family housing off post
   d. Civilian housing you own
   e. Civilian housing your rent, off post
   f. With family or friends
   g. Temporary housing (e.g., hotel, motel)

4. How long have you lived in your current location?

5. [IF SPOUSE LIVES OFF POST] Approximately how far away from your spouse's military installation do you live (in miles)?

6. At which military installation is your spouse currently stationed?

7. How long has your spouse been stationed at this installation?

8. Are you currently living in the same location as your spouse?
   a. If no: where are you currently living?

9. How many years have you been married to your current spouse?

10. Before you were married to your spouse, did you have any other exposure to the military (e.g., family member in the military)?

11. Do any children under the age of 18 live with you at least half-time? If so, how old are they?

Connections to Other Spouses and Army Community

12. To what degree do you feel you are connected with other Army spouses?
    a. Probes:
       i. How often do you communicate or interact with other Army spouses?
       ii. In what ways do you interact or engage with other Army spouses?
       iii. Are you connected with your soldier and family readiness groups? If so, please describe.
       iv. Are your connections to other Army spouses helpful to you? Why or why not?
       v. Are there ways in which you would like to be more connected with other Army spouses? If so, please describe.

13. To what degree do you feel you are connected to the Army community overall? Please explain.

14. Has your connection to the Army community varied over time? For example, was it stronger at previous garrisons than your current garrison?
    a. Probe: What made it different?

Information About Available Resources

Life sometimes creates problems or challenges for soldiers and their families. Some of those problems or challenges can include questions about military culture, work-life balance issues, household management issues, financial or legal problems, your spouse's well-being, your well-being, your children's well-being, relationship problems, and problems navigating the health care system. The Army provides programs and services to serve as resources to help with problems or challenges you and your family might face—things like recreation facilities and programs, childcare and family support programs, spiritual support, and medical care. We'll be talking mostly about resources that the military provides.

15. When you have a problem or challenge and need help or support, where do you typically go to find that help?
    a. Probe (if needed): Tell me a little more about this process. Where do you start when looking for help? What do you do next if you can't find the help you need?
    b. Probe: Do you talk or connect online with other Army spouses about where to go for help? For general social support?
    c. If you have a question or concern, either in general or about a resource you are trying to use, where do you typically go to get answers?

16. When your spouse [or child] needs help, do you seek help or information in the same way, or do you do something different?
    a. Probe (if needed): Tell me a little more about this process. Where do you start when looking for help? What do you do next if you can't find the help you need?

17. In general, how do you typically find out about resources available to you as a military spouse?
    a. Probe: Do you hear about resources
        i. by word of mouth from other spouses?
        ii. from your active duty spouse?
        iii. via formal communication from military spouse groups?
        iv. via formal communication from the Army services themselves or the installation?
    b. Probe (if not clear): Do you usually find out about resources online, by calling someone, or some other method? Is this how you prefer to find out about resources, or is there some other way you would like to be made aware of the resources available to you?

Experiences with Resources

The next questions are about a problem or challenge you've faced in the past year—one that you've sought out help for, whether you received that help or not. This could be help you sought through Army resources, civilian resources, or just through support from people you know. Take a moment to think about a problem or challenge you've faced in the past year that you sought out help for. [Wait a few seconds or more.] Got it?

18. What kind of problem was this—a problem with work-life balance, a problem with military culture, a relationship problem, a problem your child experienced, or something else?

Thinking of this problem,

19. Did you reach out to any Army or other military resources to deal with this problem?
    a. If so: Where did you first go for help?
        i. Were they able to help you with your problem?
    b. Did you seek out any other Army or military resources to address this problem? If yes: How many Army resources did you use?
        i. If you used more than one resource, why did you do so?
            1. Probes:
                a. Were your needs not met by the first resource(s) you contacted?
                b. Did you struggle to identify the appropriate resource to address your problem and have to approach several resources before finding the appropriate one for your issue?
                c. Did your problem include various components that required a variety of resources?
                d. Did your first resource refer you to other resources, or did you seek out multiple resources on your own?

  c. If not, why did you not use Army resources to address your problem or challenge?
    i. Probes:
      1. Were you not aware of the appropriate Army resource to address your problem or challenge?
      2. Did you lack confidence in Army resources' ability to address your problem or challenge?
      3. Was accessing Army resources too difficult? If so, how so?

20. Did you reach out to civilian resources for help? Things like the local library, a pastor or religious leader, friends or family, or even just the civilian internet. If so, please describe your experiences using these resources.

21. Overall, were your needs met by the resources you used? Please explain.

22. Are there certain Army resources or programs that have a good reputation in the Army spouse community? If so, what is it about those resources that contributes to them having a good reputation? What types of things are they doing well?
  a. [IF SPOUSE HAS USED ARMY RESOURCES] Would you say that you had a positive experience with the Army resources or programs you used?
    i. If so, what was it about those Army resources or programs that worked well for you? What were they doing right?
      1. Probe: Were those resources and programs
      2. respectful and friendly?
      3. easy to access (e.g., hours, location)?
      4. discreet in dealing with your situation?
      5. responsive to your concerns?

23. Similarly, are there certain Army resources or programs that have a bad reputation in the Army spouse community? If so, what is it about those resources or programs that contribute to them having a bad reputation? What types of things are they doing poorly?
  a. [IF SPOUSE REPORTED NOT HAVING A POSITIVE EXPERIENCE WITH ARMY RESOURCES IN 22a] What was it about the Army resources or programs you used that led to a negative experience for you? What about these resources needed improvement?
    i. Probe: Were those resources and programs
    ii. disrespectful or unfriendly?
    iii. difficult to access (e.g., hours, location)?
    iv. not discreet?
    v. not responsive?

24. Do you have unmet needs that Army resources or programs that you are aware of do not address or have not addressed? Please explain and describe.

Closing Questions

25. Overall, how could Army resources and programs be improved to better support your needs or to make you more likely to use these resources and programs?

    a. Overall, how could communication about Army resources and programs be improved to better inform military spouses of the support available to them?

26. Do you have any additional comments about any of the topics we discussed today, or any other final thoughts?

Additional Interview Participant Information and Qualitative Analysis Coding Guide

This appendix provides additional information on the interview methodology and a detailed description of the qualitative data coding conducted for the 42 interviews with Army spouses.

Interview Response Rates and Number of Participants

Over a two-month period (late January to March 2020), outreach through email invitation was extended to a sample of spouses of active duty Army soldiers, with the aim to conduct interviews with at least 40 spouses, to include at least 28 enlisted spouses and 12 officer spouses, and also to achieve diversity in terms of the distance of participants' housing from the military installations where their soldiers are assigned. In order to complete 40 interviews, a total of 285 individuals were invited in batches. As a result of outreach, a total of 55 spouses volunteered to participate, and 42 completed an interview, resulting in a response rate of roughly 15 percent.[1] In addition to the 55 spouses who volunteered to participate in interviews, a small number of spouses responded to the email invitation to inform the research team that they did not qualify to participate in the interview because their spouse was no longer active duty Army or they were no longer married to their active duty spouse.

Qualitative Analysis Coding Guide

The research team uploaded interview notes in transcript form into the NVivo qualitative data analysis software program, and one member of the research team who has knowledge of the substantive area and considerable experience with qualitative methods and analysis conducted the coding analysis. Coding was conducted in three phases in NVivo. The first phase involved coding all interview text according to the participants' background information as provided, such as their living situations (e.g., housing distance from military location, length

---

[1] Reasons for volunteering to participate but not completing interviews included individuals not responding to follow-up emails from the research team to schedule interview times and individuals not attending their scheduled interviews and not responding to emails to reschedule their interviews.

of time in current housing), the pay grades of participants' active duty spouses, whether or not the participants had previous exposure to the military, and whether or not they had children under 18 living in their household. (Table 2.2 in Chapter Two outlines all participant background characteristics that were included in coding.) This allowed for the identification of trends according to these background characteristics. The second phase of coding focused on high-level content coding of interview discussions based on protocol questions; this phase can be considered a sorting of comments by protocol topic area. The third phase of coding involved a deep dive into content coding, identifying key themes within each protocol topic area that emerged across interviews.

Table C.1 is a complete coding guide of the content codes for the second and third coding phases that displays how text was coded by levels of coding. Level 1 codes are the broadest codes, with levels 2, 3, and 4 becoming increasingly more specific with each level. We coded down to the most specific-level code whenever possible. The codes noted in the table correspond to the questions as numbered in the interview protocol in Appendix B. Text was coded with the most appropriate code, no matter when in the discussion or in response to which question a comment occurred. More than one code could be assigned to the same text if that comment touched on more than one theme. Nearly 100 codes were developed during the coding process.

TABLE C.1

Coding Guide for Qualitative Analysis of Interview Data

Level 1 Code	Level 2 Code	Level 3 Code	Level 4 Code	Description of Code	Corresponding Protocol Question
Connections				Comments about connections with other Army spouses and the Army community overall	Questions 12, 13, 14
	Other spouses			Comments about the degree to which participants feel connected to other Army spouses	Questions 12, 12i, 12ii
		Engaged		Comments about being engaged with other Army spouses	Questions 12, 12i, 12ii
		Little to no engagement		Comments about not being engaged with other Army spouses	Questions 12, 12i, 12ii
		Helpful		Comments related to the helpfulness of connections with other Army spouses	Question 12iv
			Yes	Comments about connections with other spouses being helpful	Question 12iv

Table C.1—Continued

Level 1 Code	Level 2 Code	Level 3 Code	Level 4 Code	Description of Code	Corresponding Protocol Question
			No	Comments about connections with other spouses not being helpful	Question 12iv
		Want more connection		Comments related to whether participants desire more connection to other Army spouses	Question 12v
			Yes	Comments about participants wanting more connection with other spouses	Question 12v
			No	Comments about participants not wanting more connection with other spouses	Question 12v
	SFRGs			Comments related to engagement level with SFRGs	Question 12iii
		SFRG engagement		Comments about being engaged with SFRGs	Question 12iii
		No SFRG engagement		Comments about not being engaged with SFRGs	Question 12iii
	Army community			Comments about the degree to which participants feel connected to the Army community overall	Question 13
		Connected		Comments about feeling connected with the Army community	Question 13
		Not connected or limited		Comments about not feeling connected with the Army community	Question 13
		Changed over time		Comments related to connections to the Army community changing over time	Question 14
			N/A first installation	Comments about no changes by location because they are at their first installation	Question 14
			Same	Comments about connections to the Army community not changing over time	Question 14

Table C.1—Continued

Level 1 Code	Level 2 Code	Level 3 Code	Level 4 Code	Description of Code	Corresponding Protocol Question
Where to typically go for help				Comments related to where participants go to find help when facing a problem or challenge	Question 15
	Active duty spouse			Comments about seeking help from their active duty spouses	Question 15
	ACS or Military OneSource			Comments about seeking help from ACS or Military OneSource	Question 15
	Other spouses			Comments about seeking help from other Army spouses (including using Facebook spouse groups)	Question 15
	Google or online searches			Comments about seeking help by using Google or other online search tools	Question 15
	Family			Comments about seeking help from family	Question 15
	SFRGs			Comments about seeking help from SFRGs	Question 15
	Other			Comments about seeking help from other sources	Question 15
	Multiple			Comments regarding spouses using multiple sources to seek help	Question 15
	Different for spouse or child			Comments related to where participants seek help for their active duty spouses or children	Question 16
How to find out about resources				Comments related to how participants typically find out about resources available to them	Question 17

Table C.1—Continued

Level 1 Code	Level 2 Code	Level 3 Code	Level 4 Code	Description of Code	Corresponding Protocol Question
	Active duty spouse			Comments about finding out about resources from their active duty spouses	Question 17
	Other spouses			Comments about finding out about resources from their other spouses (including using Facebook spouse groups)	Question 17
	Google or online searches			Comments about finding out about resources through Google or other online search tools	Question 17
	Welcome program or packets			Comments about finding out about resources through information provided in welcome programs or packets provided to those new to an installation	Question 17
	SFRGs			Comments about finding out about resources through SFRGs	Question 17
	ACS			Comments about finding out about resources through ACS	Question 17
	Mailing lists			Comments about finding out about resources through mailing lists	Question 17
	Flyers and pamphlets			Comments about finding out about resources through flyers and pamphlets	Question 17
	Advertisements			Comments about finding out about resources through advertisements	Question 17
	Other			Comments about finding out about resources through other sources	Question 17

Table C.1—Continued

Level 1 Code	Level 2 Code	Level 3 Code	Level 4 Code	Description of Code	Corresponding Protocol Question
	How prefer to find out			Comments regarding how participants would prefer to find out about resources	Question 17b
Process for specific problem				Comments regarding a specific problem participants have recently sought help for	Questions 18, 19, 20, 21
	Type of problem			Comments regarding the type of problem participants sought help for	Question 18
		Army related		Comments about problems that are Army related in nature	Question 18
		Not Army related		Comments about problems that are not Army related in nature	Question 18
		Unclear		Comments about problems where the type is unclear as to whether it is Army related or not	Question 18
	Multiple resources used or asked			Comments about participants using multiple resources to address a problem	Question 19
	Single resource used			Comments about participants using only one resource to address a problem	Question 19
	Civilian resource use			Comments regarding participants using civilian resources to address a problem	Question 20
		Yes, used		Comments about participants using civilian resources	Question 20
		No, not used		Comments about participants not using civilian resources	Question 20
	Nothing used			Comments about participants using no resources to address a problem	Questions 19, 20

Table C.1—Continued

Level 1 Code	Level 2 Code	Level 3 Code	Level 4 Code	Description of Code	Corresponding Protocol Question
	Needs met or not			Comments regarding whether participants' needs were met for the recent problem	Question 21
		Yes, met		Comments about needs related to recent problem being met	Question 21
		No, not met		Comments about needs related to recent problem not being met	Question 21
		Mixed		Comments about needs being partially met or partially not met	Question 21
Reputation of resources				Comments about the reputation of Army resources or programs in the Army spouse community	Questions 22, 23
	Good reputation programs			Comments regarding resources or programs that have a good reputation in the Army spouse community	Question 22
		ACS, MWR, USO		Comments about ACS, MWR, or USO having a good reputation	Question 22
		Childcare		Comments about childcare resources having a good reputation	Question 22
		SFRGs		Comments about SFRGs having a good reputation	Question 22
		Financial		Comments about financial services having a good reputation	Question 22
		Education		Comments about educational resources having a good reputation	Question 22
		Other		Comments about other programs that have a good reputation	Question 22

Table C.1—Continued

Level 1 Code	Level 2 Code	Level 3 Code	Level 4 Code	Description of Code	Corresponding Protocol Question
		Qualities of good programs		Comments about what qualities make programs or resources "good"	Question 22a
	Bad-reputation programs			Comments regarding resources or programs that have a bad reputation in the Army spouse community	Question 23
		None		Comments about there being no programs or resources that have a bad reputation	Question 23
		Childcare		Comments about childcare having a bad reputation	Question 23
		Employment		Comments about employment resources having a bad reputation	Question 23
		SFRG		Comments about SFRGs having a bad reputation	Question 23
		Housing		Comments about military housing resources having a bad reputation	Question 23
		Medical		Comments about the Army medical system having a bad reputation	Question 23
		Other		Comments about other resources that have a bad reputation	Question 23
		Qualities of bad programs		Comments about what qualities make programs or resources "bad"	Question 23a
Unmet needs				Comments regarding any unmet needs that Army programs or resources do not address	Question 24
	None			Comments about participants not having any unmet needs	Question 24

Table C.1—Continued

Level 1 Code	Level 2 Code	Level 3 Code	Level 4 Code	Description of Code	Corresponding Protocol Question
	Employment			Comments about participants having unmet needs related to employment	Question 24
	Mental health or counseling			Comments about participants having unmet needs related to mental health or counseling services	Question 24
	Other			Comments about participants having other types of unmet needs	Question 24
Improvements				Comments regarding improvements to Army resources or programs or to communication about resources	Questions 25 and 25a
	Resources and programs			Comments regarding improvements to Army resources or programs to better support needs or make spouses more likely to use	Question 25
		Childcare		Comments about improvements to childcare resources	Question 25
		Employment		Comments about improvements to employment resources	Question 25
		For deployment		Comments about improvements to resources for spouses during active duty member deployments	Question 25
		Medical		Comments about improvements to the Army medical system	Question 25
		Customer service		Comments about improvements to resource staff customer service	Question 25
		Timing and accessibility		Comments about improvements to the timing and accessibility (e.g., hours/days open) of resources	Question 25

Table C.1—Continued

Level 1 Code	Level 2 Code	Level 3 Code	Level 4 Code	Description of Code	Corresponding Protocol Question
		Other		Comments about other types of improvements to resources	Question 25
	Communication			Comments regarding improvements to the communication of Army resources and programs to better inform spouses	Question 25a
		Better marketing		Comments about improvements to how resources are marketed	Question 25a
		Centralized information repository		Comments about creating improved centralized resource information repositories	Question 25a
		Welcome information better		Comments about improving welcome information or welcome programs when new to an installation	Question 25a
		Other		Comments about other ways to improve communication of resources	Question 25a
Additional comments				Additional comments provided outside protocol question content	N/A
Of note				Particularly pertinent comment or quote (use sparingly)	N/A

References

American Psychological Association, Presidential Task Force on Military Deployment Services for Youth, Families and Service Members, *The Psychological Needs of U.S. Military Service Members and Their Families: A Preliminary Report*, Washington, D.C.: American Psychological Association, 2007.

Bowen, Gary L., Todd M. Jensen, James A. Martin, and Jay A. Mancini, "The Willingness of Military Members to Seek Help: The Role of Social Involvement and Social Responsibility," *American Journal of Community Psychology*, Vol. 57, Nos. 1–2, 2016, pp. 203–215.

Bowen, Gary L., Jay A. Mancini, James A. Martin, William B. Ware, and John P. Nelson, "Promoting the Adaptation of Military Families: An Empirical Test of a Community Practice Model," *Family Relations*, Vol. 52, No. 1, 2003, pp. 33–44.

Burrell, Lolita M., Doris Briley Durand, and Jennifer Fortado, "Military Community Integration and Its Effect on Well-Being and Retention," *Armed Forces & Society*, Vol. 30, No. 1, 2003, pp. 7–24.

Chewning, Lisa V., and Beth Montemurro, "The Structure of Support: Mapping Network Evolution in an Online Support Group," *Computers in Human Behavior*, Vol. 64, 2016, pp. 355–365.

Cohen, Sheldon, and Thomas A. Wills, "Stress, Social Support, and the Buffering Hypothesis," *Psychological Bulletin*, Vol. 98, No. 2, 1985, pp. 310–357.

Cooper, Cary L., Philip J. Dewe, and Michael P. O'Driscoll, *Organizational Stress: A Review and Critique of Theory, Research, and Applications*, Thousand Oaks, Calif.: Sage, 2001.

Cornwell, E. Y., and L. J. Waite, "Social Disconnectedness, Perceived Isolation, and Health Among Older Adults," *Journal of Health and Social Behavior*, Vol. 50, No. 1, 2009, pp. 31–48.

Defense Manpower Data Center, *2015 Survey of Active Duty Spouses: Tabulations of Responses*, Alexandria, Va., 2016, Report 2015-028.

Folkman, Susan, Richard S. Lazarus, Christine Dunkel-Schetter, Anita DeLongis, and Rand J. Gruen, "Dynamics of a Stressful Encounter: Cognitive Appraisal, Coping, and Encounter Outcomes," *Journal of Personality and Social Psychology*, Vol. 50, No. 5, 1986, pp. 992–1003.

Granovetter, Mark, "Small Is Bountiful: Labor Markets and Establishment Size," *American Sociological Review*, Vol. 49, No. 3, 1984, pp. 323–334.

Hawkins, Stacy A., Annie Condon, Jacob N. Hawkins, Kristine Liu, Yxsel Melendrez Ramirez, Marisa M, Nihill, and Jackson Tolins, *What We Know About Military Family Readiness: Evidence from 2007–2017*, Washington, D.C.: Office of the Deputy Under Secretary of the Army, 2018.

Hill, Reuben, Elise Boulding, and Lowell Dunigan, *Families Under Stress*, New York: Harper and Row, 1949.

Hughes, M. E., L. J. Waite, L. C. Hawkley, and J. T. Cacioppo, "A Short Scale for Measuring Loneliness in Large Surveys: Results From Two Population-Based Studies," *Research on Aging*, Vol. 26, No. 6, 2004, pp. 655–672.

Lewandowski, Joshua, Benjamin D. Rosenberg, M. Jordan Parks, and Jason T. Siegel, "The Effect of Informal Social Support: Face-to-Face Versus Computer-Mediated Communication," *Computers in Human Behavior*, Vol. 27, No. 5, 2011, pp. 1806–1814.

Lucier-Greer, Mallory, Catherine W. O'Neal, A. Laura Arnold, Jay A. Mancini, and Kandauda K. A. S. Wickrama, "Adolescent Mental Health and Academic Functioning: Empirical Support for Contrasting Models of Risk and Vulnerability," *Military Medicine*, Vol. 179, No. 11, 2014, pp. 1279–1287.

McCubbin, Hamilton I., and Joan M. Patterson, "The Family Stress Process: The Double ABCX Model of Adjustment and Adaptation," *Marriage and Family Review*, Vol. 6, Nos. 1–2, 1983, pp. 7–37.

Military OneSource, "Welcome to Military INSTALLATIONS," web database, undated. As of August 18, 2021:
https://installations.militaryonesource.mil/

National Academies of Sciences, Engineering, and Medicine, *Strengthening the Military Family Readiness System for a Changing American Society*, Washington, D.C.: National Academies Press, 2019.

Office of the Assistant Chief of Staff for Installation Management, "Soldier and Family Readiness Groups," webpage, August 16, 2019. As of August 18, 2021:
https://www.army.mil/standto/archive_2019-08-16/

O'Neal, Catherine Walker, Jacquelyn K. Mallette, and Jay A. Mancini, "The Importance of Parents' Community Connections for Adolescent Well-Being: An Examination of Military Families," *American Journal of Community Psychology*, Vol. 61, Nos. 1–2, 2018, pp. 204–217.

Richardson, Evin W., Jacquelyn K. Mallette, Catherine W. O'Neal, and Jay A. Mancini, "Do Youth Development Programs Matter? An Examination of Transitions and Well-Being Among Military Youth," *Journal of Child and Family Studies*, Vol. 25, No. 6, 2016, pp. 1765–1776.

Sims, Carra S., Thomas E. Trail, Emily K. Chen, Erika Meza, Parisa Roshan, and Beth E. Lachman, *Assessing the Needs of Soldiers and Their Families at the Garrison Level*, Santa Monica, Calif.: RAND Corporation, RR-2148-A, 2018. As of August 18, 2021:
https://www.rand.org/pubs/research_reports/RR2148.html

Sims, Carra S., Thomas E. Trail, Emily K. Chen, and Laura L. Miller, *Today's Soldier: Assessing the Needs of Soldiers and Their Families*, Santa Monica, Calif.: RAND Corporation, RR-1893-A, 2017. As of May 21, 2020:
https://www.rand.org/pubs/research_reports/RR1893.html

Taylor, Shelley E., "Social Support: A Review," in Howard S. Friedman, ed., *The Oxford Handbook of Health Psychology*, New York: Oxford University Press, 2011, pp. 189–214.

Trail, Thomas E., Carra S. Sims, and Margaret Tankard, *Today's Army Spouse Survey: How Army Families Address Life's Challenges*, Santa Monica, Calif.: RAND Corporation, RR-3224-A, 2019. As of August 18, 2021:
https://www.rand.org/pubs/research_reports/RR3224.html

Wellman, Barry, and Scot Wortley, "Different Strokes from Different Folks: Community Ties and Social Support," *American Journal of Sociology*, Vol. 96, No. 3, 1990, pp. 558–588.